The Romance of Creative Healthy Cookery

The Romance of Creative Healthy Cookery

by William and Trudy Fischer

Fischer Publishing
Canfield, Ohio 44406

ISBN 0-915421-11-9
Printed in the United States of America

FISCHER PUBLISHING CORPORATION
Canfield, Oh 44406

To all Health Conscious People

These recipes, created with attention to a healthy lifestyle, provide a delicious way to improve your sense of well being. Our purpose in writing this book is to help people lead healthier, happier lives.

Special thanks to the many people who offered assistance and gave encouragement while we were writing this book.

Introduction

At Fischer Publishing our focus remains consistent. We believe in good health!

We advocate taking charge of your life to maintain your good health or to regain it if you have lost it through poor habits or through illness. It is our belief that active participation in your body's health will prevent illness and give you a tremendous feeling of physical and psychological well-being.

One of the ways in which you can take charge of your health is by adopting good nutritional habits. That is the purpose of this cookbook.

All of the recipes call for healthy, natural ingredients, and whenever possible we have tried to suggest low calorie or low cholesterol ways to prepare these foods. Our main dishes are fish and fowl; no red meat is suggested. In addition, we have prepared wonderful selections of soups, salads, hors d'oeuvres and delicious all-natural desserts.

As adults, few of us drink as much milk or eat enough dairy foods to get the calcium our bones so desperately need. For that reason, we have added a bonus to this cookbook—recipes made with wholesome, healthy natural cheeses.

Remember that moderation in all things is important. Keep your diet balanced, control your intake of calories, exercise at least four times each week, avoid alcohol and cigarettes and eat red meat no more than twice a week. The results will be wonderful!

Here's to your very good health!

Sincerely,

William Fischer

TABLE OF CONTENTS

BREAKFAST

Research over the last few years has determined that breakfast is the single most important meal of the day. A balanced, nutritional breakfast gets the metabolism going, provides sustained energy for the workday ahead and has even been shown to significantly improve the performance of schoolchildren.

Unfortunately, in our time-oriented society, a cup of coffee and a donut has become the typical American breakfast, but a good breakfast need not be time-consuming. Whole grain breads and muffins and commercial cereals containing nuts, fruits and whole grains can provide the sustained carbohydrate energy needed to start the day.

Accompany whole grains with a piece of fruit or a glass of juice, and you have a healthy, quick breakfast.

On the days when you do have time to fix, consider one of these delicious recipes.

EGGS

Golden yellow, delicious and nutritious, eggs can be fixed in a variety of palate-pleasing recipes. While it is true that eggs, particularly the yolks, are high in cholesterol, research has now shown that the body itself can produce more cholesterol independent of substances which contain it. Eggs are high in protein, taste delicious and are naturally low in calories. The best rule to follow is the rule of moderation. Don't eat eggs every day—vary the diet. But when you do eat them, try some of the unique recipes offered here.

A Few Egg Tips

—To prevent eggs from over-boiling and cracking, add a dash of salt and a squirt of vinegar to the water.

—Stick a needle through the two pointed ends of the egg before cooking; air will escape and the eggs will not crack as easily.

—Cool eggs in cold water for easier shelling.

FARMER'S OMELETTE

3 slices bacon	1½ oz. cheese
1 pat butter	6 tbsps. milk
mixed chopped vegetables	pepper
(carrots, leeks, cauliflower,	ground paprika
peas or 1 can succotash)	seasoned salt
salt	tomato
thyme	parsley
6 eggs	

Cut bacon into small pieces and fry in butter until crisp. Saute finely chopped vegetables in the same pan for five minutes, then season with salt and thyme. Beat eggs, stir in grated cheese, milk and other seasonings. Cook omelette in a second frying pan until eggs are set, then slip omelette onto a warmed plate, spoon vegetables and bacon over half and fold over second half. Garnish with slices of tomato and parsley.

OMELETTE LORRAINE

4 slices whole wheat bread	6 oz. aged cheese
3 slices bacon	1½ oz. young cheese
6 eggs	parsley
6 tablespoons milk	lettuce

Cut bread and bacon into small pieces and fry them until golden brown. Beat eggs and milk, pour them over the bread and bacon and cook until the eggs are half set. Cover with slices of young cheese and continue cooking until the eggs are set. Sprinkle with grated old cheese, finely chopped parsley and serve on lettuce leaves.

EGGS JOSEPHINE

dash vinegar	1½ oz. ham
4 eggs	1½ oz. aged cheese
pat butter	salt
1 tbsp. flour	pepper
1¼ c. milk	oregano
1 egg	parsley

Bring water with dash of vinegar to a boil. Break the eggs into the boiling water, gently retain their shape with two spoons while poaching gently for 3 minutes. Remove from water, drain and place in ovenproof dish. Make a smooth sauce with melted butter, flour and milk, stirring continuously. Complete the sauce by stirring in a beaten egg, chopped ham, grated cheese (reserve a little for the garnish), salt and seasonings. Pour the sauce over the poached eggs, sprinkle with the grated cheese put aside for this purpose and place the dish under the broiler until the cheese is golden brown.

EGGS IN THE NEST

2 slices bacon	nutmeg
1 onion	thyme
2 whole tomatoes	ground paprika
salt, pepper	chives
4 eggs	parsley
¼ c. milk	1½ oz. aged cheese

Fry bacon until crisp. Add onion, sliced into rings and saute in bacon fat. Put bacon and onion in a flat oven-proof dish. Remove skins from tomatoes by pouring boiling water over them. Cut them into quarters and season with salt and pepper. Beat the eggs with the milk, salt, seasonings, finely chopped chives and parsley. Arrange the tomato quarters on the bacon and onion mixture, and pour over the egg and milk. Cover with grated cheese and place the dish for about 15 minutes in a preheated oven (375 degrees) until eggs are firm and the cheese has turned golden brown.

INDIVIDUAL GOUDA EGGS

1 tbsp. butter
½ c. fresh mushrooms
½ mature Gouda cheese, grated
pepper
4 eggs

Wash mushrooms, cut into leaves and saute in butter for 5 minutes. Butter 4 small glass bowls, put in a layer of grated mature Gouda, pepper lightly and set an egg onto each. Garnish the mushroom around the yolks and cover with a layer of Gouda cheese. Set the bowls into the oven and let the eggs harden to desired consistency for 5–12 minutes.

STUFFED EGGS "ALKMAAR"

4 large, hard-boiled eggs
½ c. fresh Gouda cheese, grated
3–4 tbsp. condensed milk
1 tsp. mustard
pepper
parsley

Run eggs through cold water after boiling; remove the shells and let cool. Cut eggs in half lengthwise and remove the yolks without damaging the whites. Blend the yolks, grated cheese, condensed milk and the seasonings until a foamy cream develops. Season to taste, and spoon onto egg halves. Garnish with parsley, and serve on lettuce leaves.

POACHED EGGS

4 large, round rolls	½ cup cream cheese
1 tbsp. mayonnaise	4 eggs
1 tbsp. ketchup	pinch of salt
½ c. shrimp, frozen or canned	paprika
	2 sprigs parsley

Cut off the top of the rolls; remove the soft inner white bread and spread the inside with a mixture of mayonnaise and ketchup. Layer the shrimp and cubed cream cheese evenly in the rolls. Lay an egg in the center of each roll and bake in a pre-heated oven at 300 degrees for 5–8 minutes, or broil for a few minutes, until the egg white is hardened. Season lightly with salt and paprika and garnish with chopped parsley. Serve immediately.

SHORESIDE SOUFFLE

3 tbsp. butter	5 oz canned mushrooms
2 tbsp. flour	1 cup aged Gouda cheese
1 cup milk	4 eggs divided
7 oz. shrimp, frozen or canned	dash of salt
	curry

Melt the butter, add flour and saute the flour until light yellow. Pour in the milk and let boil up thoroughly. Drain the shrimp, cut the mushroom into leaves, cube the cheese, and blend all into the thick sauce. Bind with the beaten egg yolk, season to taste and finally blend in the stiffly beaten egg white. Pour the entire mixture into a greased, heat-resistant pan and bake for 30–35 minutes at 350 degrees.

FLUFFY FILLED CHEESE OMELETTES

*For 4 six-inch omelettes or 2 twelve-inch omelettes

Filling:	Omelette Mixture:
2 tbsp. butter	4 egg yolks
1 onion	2 tbsp. cream
1 can peeled Italian tomatoes	¼ c. aged Gouda cheese, grated
pepper	pinch of paprika
salt	dash of white pepper
1 bunch chives	6 egg whites
	butter

Melt the butter and stew the diced onion until glazed. Add the tomatoes in their own liquid, season with salt and pepper. Let it cook for a few minutes. Dice the chives, blend in with the tomato mixture, season to taste and keep on low heat.

Lightly beat the yolks with a fork; add the cream, grated Gouda cheese and seasonings. Beat the egg whites until stiff, blend into the yolk mixture, and cook immediately. Heat butter in the frying pan, not letting the butter turn brown. Pour in the frothy mixture. Cover, and let the omelettes set in low heat. The bottom of the omelette should be golden yellow. Pour a little tomato mush over half of it, and fold the other half over. Glide the omelette onto a pre-warmed plate.

EGG IN CHEESE-HERB SAUCE

8 eggs	½ cup cream cheese
2 small packages light gravy	½ bunch parsley
1 cup water	½ bunch chives
1 cup milk	1 sprig dill
1 egg yolk	

Boil the eggs until they are soft, about 4–5 minutes. Warm the water and milk and, stirring constantly, pour in the contents of the gravy packages. Let boil up thoroughly and uncover. Bind with yolks and blend with the cubed cream cheese. The cheese should be completely dissolved. Add the finely-chopped herbs, season the sauce to taste, and pour into a pre-warmed dish. Lay the halved eggs into it.

SAVOY OMELETTES

3 tbsp. butter	1 green pepper
3 oz. smoked lean bacon	⅔ cup baby Gouda cheese
3 medium boiled potatoes	8 eggs
1 red pepper	pinch of salt
	dash of peppermill
	½ bunch parsley

Heat butter in a frying pan, cook the cubed bacon until glazed. Cut the boiled potatoes into small cubes. Wash the peppers and cut into strips; put into the frying pan and braise for 5–8 minutes. Cube the Gouda cheese into ½ inch cubes. Combine eggs, seasonings, and chopped parsley, pour over the potatoes, fork through until set. As soon as the bottom turns light brown, pour the mixture over the surface that is still soft and runny. Fold over one half and serve immediately.

FLUFFY OMELETTES WITH FRUIT

*For 4 six-inch omelettes or 2 twelve-inch omelettes

Omelette mixture:	Filling:
6 egg yolks	1 4–6 oz. jar cherries
pinch of salt	1 4–6 oz. can peaches
dash of grated lemon peel	
½ cup sugar	
6 egg whites	
½ cup powdered sugar	
butter	

Lightly beat the egg yolks, add the salt, lemon peel and sugar, and blend well. Beat the egg whites until stiff and blend into the egg yolk mixture. For best results cook immediately using 2 frying pans. Heat the butter, lower the heat, and pour in a portion of the frothy mixture. Cover, and let the mixture fluff up on the lowest heat setting for 8–10 minutes. The omelettes have to be well-done and golden yellow on the bottom. Cover one half with drained cherries and peach wedges. Fold over the other half and dust with powdered sugar.

EGG CREAMS

4 eggs	seasoned salt
4 tbsps. coffee cream	chives
(or evaporated milk)	butter
4 tbsps. water	cooked rice
salt	tomato or madeira sauce
pepper	

Whisk the eggs with the coffee, milk, water and seasonings, and chill in the refrigerator. Beat until foamy and pour into buttered pudding molds or small fire-proof dishes, which should only be filled three-quarters full. Place the dishes in a pre-heated oven (325 degrees) for about 30 minutes until the egg creams are firm and light golden brown. Pile the cooked rice into the center of a heated serving dish, unmold the egg creams, arrange them around the rice and serve the tomato or madeira sauce separately. (Pour a little over the rice for garnish.)

CHEESE SOUFFLE

2 tbsps. butter	thyme
2 tbsps. flour	3 eggs
1¼ cup milk	1½ oz. grated cheese
salt and pepper	1½ oz. ham
ground paprika	2 tbsps. madeira
worcestershire sauce	butter
tabasco sauce	

Make a smooth creamy sauce with the butter, flour, milk and seasonings. Separate the eggs and stir a little of the sauce into the beaten egg yolks. Pour back into the sauce, stir in the grated cheese, the shredded ham and the madeira—taste to check the flavor. Beat the egg whites until very stiff and carefully fold them into the sauce. Pour the mixture into a buttered oven-proof dish (1 quart) which should not be filled to more than two-thirds full. Place in the lower part of a pre-heated oven (400 degrees). Bake for about 30 minutes until well-risen and golden brown. Heat the lid of the dish in the oven. Serve the souffle immediately covered with the warm lid.

CARAWAY-SCRAMBLED EGGS

4 eggs	1 tsp. caraway seed
2 tbsp. water or cream	½ cup grated Gouda
dash of salt	2 tbsps. butter for frying
pepper	

Whisk the eggs with the desired liquid, salt and pepper. Add caraway and grated Gouda cheese. Heat the butter in a frying pan until hot, but don't let it turn brown. Pour in the eggs, tilt the pan a little to the side and run the eggs through with a fork when the egg is set on the bottom. Keep cooking until all is set.

COUNTRY DISH

5 eggs	½ cup smoked lean bacon
1 cup cream	2 onions
pinch of salt	1 cup aged Gouda cheese
peppermill	1 bunch chives
¼ cup breadcrumbs	1 tbsp. butter

Whisk the eggs, cream, salt and pepper. Cut the bacon into small cubes and lay out on a flat, heat-resistant pan. Add thinly-diced onions and stew until glazed. Cube the Gouda cheese and add them together with the finely chopped chives into the pan. Combine well. Pour the egg mixture over it, and let it set for 8 minutes in a pre-heated oven at 400 degrees. Briefly remove the pan, dot with butter, sprinkle with breadcrumbs. Use the remaining butter to form flakes over the breadcrumbs. Bake until golden yellow for 5 minutes. Slice and serve with rye bread.

OMELETTE SURPRISE

Biscuit Dough:	Meringue:
4 tbsp. butter	3 egg whites
3 eggs, divided	¾ cup sugar
¾ cup sugar	1 pint vanilla ice cream
pinch of salt	
¾ cup flour	
¼ level tsp. baking powder	
2–4 tbsp. cherry liquor (Kirsch)	

Melt the butter and let it cool. Whip the egg yolks with ¾ of the sugar until foamy. Beat the egg yolks with the remaining sugar and pinch of salt until stiff, and pour over the egg yolk cream. Combine the flour with the baking powder and sift over it. Pour in the butter and whisk everything well. Lay a sheet of tinfoil over a pan and spread the dough on top.

The biscuit crust should be twice the size of the Pyrex that you use for broiling the omelettes. Bake the dough in a pre-heated oven at 400 degrees for 10–13 minutes until light yellow; remove and place on a sheet of tinfoil sprinkled with sugar; remove the tinfoil, cut the crust in half, sprinkle with drops of cherry liquor (Kirsch), and let cool thoroughly.

Beat the egg white with sugar until stiff. Lay one half of the biscuit crust in a large rectangular Pyrex dish. Slice the ice cream and lay on top. Cover with the second half of the crust. Coat heavily with the meringue mixture or use a decorating gun. Briefly broil the omelette under the pre-heated broiler, until the meringue turns golden-yellow.

SPICY EGGS JULISCHKA

1 large onion	4 eggs
3–4 green peppers	salt
4 peeled tomatoes	½ tsp. paprika powder
2 tbsp. butter	⅔ cup cubed Gouda cheese
4 oz. can mushrooms	

Dice the onions. Halve the peppers, remove the pulp and white ribs. Scald the tomatoes, remove, and cut into eighths. Stew the onions and tomatoes in heated butter until done. Cut the mushrooms into leaves and blend into the onions and tomatoes. Whisk the eggs with the seasonings, and add the cubed Gouda cheese; pour the mixture over the vegetables. Lift the eggs with a fork 1–2 times and let it slowly set.

OLIVE EGG DISH

butter for frying	8 anchovy fillets
1 large onion	4 eggs
1½ lbs. boiled potatoes	peppermill
2 small Vienna sausages	½ bunch parsley
1 small jar green olives	½ cup middle-aged Gouda

Heat the butter in a large frying pan. Slice the potatoes and sausages, drain and halve the olives, separate the anchovies, cut the onion into rings, and add all into the pan. Lightly stir with a spatula and flip over. Beat the eggs with pepper, blend in the chopped parsley and pour over the ingredients. Let cook on the lowest temperature for 8 minutes. Cut the Gouda cheese into strips and lay over the mixture. Cover, and let it cook for a few minutes, until the cheese begins to melt.

EGG AND MUSHROOM FRICASSEE

1¼ oz. butter	salt, pepper
1 tsp. curry powder	white wine
1¼ oz. flour	3 oz. mushrooms
1¼ oz. soup stock	4 eggs
2 tbsps. cream	

Melt the butter, stir in the curry powder and flour. Add the stock, stirring continuously, until the sauce is smooth and thick. Cook for a few minutes and then stir in the cream. Season to taste with the salt, pepper and white wine. Cut the mushrooms in half and cook them in a little salted water for 5 minutes. Stir into the sauce, together with the chopped hardboiled eggs.

EGGS A LA ROSSINI

5 eggs	2 tbsp. butter
salt and pepper	3 oz. coffee cream
1½ oz. aged cheese	

Beat the egg whites very stiff with a little salt and pepper, and spoon them into a large buttered ovenproof dish. Arrange the egg yolks on top. Cover with the grated cheese. Dot with butter. Place the dish in a preheated oven (400 degrees) for about 15 minutes. Season the cream with salt and pepper and pour this over the eggs. Return to the oven for a minute or two. Serve with spinach.

OMELETTES FLORENTINE

Omelette Mixture:	Filling:
3 oz. smoked, lean bacon	2 tbsp. butter
1 tbsp. butter	1 pkg. (10 oz.) frozen spinach
3 oz. middle-aged Gouda	dash of salt
8 eggs	nutmeg
1 tbsp. condensed milk	1 tbsp. water
butter for frying	

Bring the butter, together with the spinach, salt, nutmeg, and water to a boil; cover until the spinach is loosened. Cut the bacon into strips and fry in the butter until glazed. Cube the Gouda cheese. Whisk the eggs with milk well; add the cooked bacon strips and cheese cubes. Heat the butter in the frying pan, pour in ¼ or ½ of the omelette mixture. Lift up the eggs with the spatula or fork as they become done on the bottom. Let it set slowly. The center should still be tender and soft. When the bottom turns golden yellow, pour the filling on one half, and fold over the other half. Put the omelette on a pre-warmed plate. Cook the rest of the omelettes and serve immediately.

PANCAKES AND CEREALS

The pancake has a reputation which it certainly does not deserve. Far from being fattening, a single pancake has only 60 calories, is low in fat and high in the complex carbohydrates which can provide energy. When you combine pancakes with the fruits and vegetables in the recipes here, you have a nutritious, high-energy breakfast. Do go light on the butter and syrup, however. Try dressing pancakes with fruit and honey instead.

Cereals have come into their own in the last few years. There are now many good commercial cereals which are low in salt and sugar, have added fruits and nuts, provide high-energy, complex carbohydrates and taste delicious in the bargain. Cereals can also provide the fiber that helps our systems to regulate themselves. The delicious homemade cereals offered here add fruit and fiber to the diet and are popular staples in the European diet.

SWEET, MINI BUCKWHEAT CAKES

2 tbsp. butter	2 cups milk
1 cup buckwheat grains	2 tbsp. raisins
2 cups water	3 small apples
3 tbsp. flour	cinnamon sugar
pinch salt	
4 eggs	

Heat the butter in a casserole dish. Brown the buckwheat, add water, and let simmer in low heat for 10 minutes. Quickly cool the mixture at an open window and blend in the flour, salt, sugar and eggs. Wash the raisins and cut the apples into ½ inch cubes, and blend them into the casserole dish.

Heat the butter in the frying pan, and with a tablespoon, spoon in the dough made for 4–5 small cakes and slowly cook until light brown on both sides. Keep on a warm plate until all cakes are made. Before serving, sprinkle with cinnamon sugar.

SCRAMBLED PANCAKES

5 eggs divided	grated ½ lemon peel
⅓ cup sugar	1 cup raisins
1 cup flour	butter for frying
½ cup milk	2 tbsps. sugar
4 tbsp. butter	
salt	

Blend the egg yolks with sugar until foamy. Gradually add the flour and milk. Add the melted butter, salt and lemon peel. Finally blend in the washed and dried raisins, and fold in the stiffly beaten egg whites.

In a large frying pan, heat butter, add the batter, cook lightly, turn over, and divide immediately into 1½ inch large pieces with two forks. Cook the scrambled pancakes until golden yellow, sprinkle with sugar and serve with stewed apples or apple sauce.

STUFFED CHEESE PANCAKES

2½ oz. flour	¾ oz. Bluefort cheese
1¼ cup milk	1 oz. aged cheese
2 eggs	pepper
salt	ground paprika
3 tbsps. butter	toothpicks
2 packets cream cheese	

Make a smooth batter with the flour, milk, eggs and salt. Melt the butter (do not allow it to brown), cool a little and stir this in the batter. Fry the pancakes in an unbuttered pan. Fill at once with the cream cheese spread, made by creaming the cream cheese with the bluefort cheese, grated old cheese, pepper and ground paprika. Close the ends of the pancakes with cocktail sticks. Place in an ovenproof dish and put into a preheated oven (400 degrees) for 10 minutes.

SALZBURG DUMPLINGS

3 tbsp. butter	3 tbsp. butter for baking
¼ cup powdered sugar	4 tbsp. milk for baking
5 eggs, divided	dash of powdered sugar
1 tbsp. vanilla	
2 heaping tbsps. flour	

Sift the powdered sugar and blend with the butter and 5 egg yolks until a thick cream develops. Beat the egg whites until stiff, and finally add the vanilla sugar. Pour the beaten egg whites over the cream. Sift the flour over that, and whisk everything carefully. Add the butter and milk in a heat-resistant pan. Pour in the mixture and let it raise well in a pre-heated oven at 400 degrees for 15 minutes, until golden-yellow. Divide into portions with a tablespoon, sprinkle lightly with powdered sugar and serve immediately.

CREPES SUZETTES

*For 4 or 8 crepes:

Crepes batter:	For flaming:
¾ cup flour	3—4 oranges
3 eggs	1 lemon
1 cup milk	1 tbsp. butter
3 tbsp. butter	10 sugar cubes
pinch of salt	3—4 shots Grand Marnier
butter for frying	2—3 shots brandy or cognac

Sift the flour into a bowl, and work the eggs, milk, melted butter and salt to a smooth batter. Heat the butter, keep the pan tilted a little, pour in the batter and cook wafer-thin pancakes until golden-yellow. Lay the pancakes on top of each other and keep warm. Wash the citrus fruits under warm water, dry off, and rub with sugar cubes. Squeeze the fruit and pour the juice through a sieve. Melt the butter in a copper-coated pan on a spirit burner. Add the sugar cubes and let dissolve, continuously stirring. Pour in the fruit juice and cook halfway through. Add the Grand Marnier. Lay the crepes in the syrup one at a time, flip them over, fold up twice and arrange in a circular shape in the pan. Pour cognac over the crepes, keep the pan tilted over the spirit flames and ignite the alcohol.

PANCAKE PARADISE
(ONE BATTER, FOUR VARIATIONS)

Pancake Batter for 6–7 pancakes:

3 eggs
2 cups milk
pinch of salt
1 cup flour
butter for frying

Whisk the eggs, milk and salt. Sift the flour over the mixture and whisk until smooth. Let it simmer for a few minutes. Heat the butter in the frying pan, scoop the batter into the pan using a small scooper, and fry until golden brown on both sides.

Variations

VEGETABLE PANCAKES

1 package frozen peas (10 oz.)	pinch of sugar
2 tbsp. butter	1 tsp. corn starch
2 tbsp. water	1 can cut asparagus (4 oz.)
from canned asparagus	
dash of salt	½ bunch parsley

Stew the peas in butter and asparagus water with the seasonings for 8–10 minutes. Mix the cornstarch with a little asparagus water, and add to the peas, letting the moisture thicken. Drain the asparagus well and add to the mixture. Sprinkle with chopped parsley and lay on the pancakes; roll up or fold over.

TOMATO PANCAKES

1 tbsp. butter	pepper
1 large onion	½ cup grated Gouda cheese
1½ lbs. tomatoes	½ bunch parsley
salt	

In a frying pan, heat the butter and saute the onions until golden yellow. Slice the tomatoes and stew with the onions for 2–3 minutes, and season. Top with the coarsely-grated Gouda cheese and let it melt. Spoon 3 tbsp. of the mixture over each pancake, sprinkle with chopped parsley and serve.

HUNTER PANCAKES

3 oz. smoked lean bacon
2 lb. mushrooms
½ cup Gouda cheese
1 bunch parsley

Cut the bacon into small cubes, and the mushrooms into leaves. Grate the Gouda cheese. Dice the parsley, and combine everything together. Top each pancake with 3 tbsp. of this mixture, and fry both sides until golden brown.

FLORENTINE PANCAKES

1 package frozen spinach	pepper
(10–15 oz.)	dash of salt
2 tbsp. butter	1–2 tbsp. water
nutmeg	

In a pot, add the unthawed spinach along with all ingredients, and bring to a boil on low heat. The spinach must be loosened. Cook very thin pancakes from the batter. Spoon 2–3 tbsp. spinach onto the center of each pancake, roll up and lay side-by-side on a preheated plate.

CEREALS

APRICOT PORRIDGE

1 quart milk
2½ oz. oatmeal
¼ cup brown sugar
4 oz. dried apricots

Make a thick porridge with the milk and oats or buy ready-made oatmeal and heat it. Serve in four bowls, sprinkle with sugar and top with apricots that have been soaked in cold water overnight.

BUTTERMILK PORRIDGE WITH PRUNES

1 quart buttermilk
2½ oz. oatmeal
4 oz. prunes
syrup or molasses

Heat the oatmeal, stirring continuously. Stir in the prunes, which can be cooked for a few minutes if desired and then cut into manageable pieces. Serve with syrup or molasses.

BUCKWHEAT PORRIDGE

2½ oz. buckwheat flakes	or
1 quart milk	1 oz. buckwheat flakes
or	1 quart yogurt
2 oz. buckwheat flakes	brown sugar or honey
1 quart buttermilk	

Sprinkle the buckwheat flakes into porridge bowls. Pour milk, buttermilk or yogurt on top. Stir thoroughly and sweeten to taste with brown sugar or honey.

BIRCHER MUESLI

* This is the original European muesli mix that is so much a part of the European diet. You may substitute pears, prunes or whatever fruit suits your taste.

3 tbsps. condensed milk	2 tbsps. oat flakes
9 tbsps. water	2 large sweet apples
3 tbsps. lemon juice	chopped nuts

Mix the condensed milk, water, lemon juice and oat flakes in a bowl and stir well. Place a grater over the bowl and grate the well-washed, unpeeled apples. Stir the apple through the muesli. Spoon into four bowls and sprinkle chopped nuts on top.

YOGURT MUESLI

1½ oz. instant oatmeal	2 oz. raisins
1 pint yogurt	juice of ½ lemon
2 sweet apples	2 tbsps. honey

Stir the oat flakes through the yogurt. Grate the well-washed, unpeeled apples into the muesli and stir in the raisins, lemon juice and honey.

LUNCH AND BRUNCH

In a fast-paced culture like ours, we barely have the time to eat lunch. When we do, we often opt for the fast-food lunch in which the beef, the fish, the chicken and even the french fries are prepared by frying them in fat.

While it is not always possible to prepare a lunch, on the days when you do have time, you might consider one of the snacks, pizzas and sandwiches in this section. Many of the unusual sandwiches contain high protein, very little fat and high-energy carbohydrates. Some of them can be made the night before and then refrigerated or microwaved at the office.

A slice of pizza and a glass of fruit juice or milk also makes a highly nutritious lunch with pizza providing nutrients from the bread, meat and vegetable groups and also providing high energy carbohydrates.

You might also wish to turn to the salad section later on in the cookbook for salads which you could make ahead and then take in portions to work.

A healthy lunch, like a healthy breakfast, fuels the workday.

OPEN-FACE SANDWICHES

Bread Tips

—Keep bread in the freezer for maximum freshness, in the refrigerator if you plan to use it quickly. This is especially true for whole-grain breads which do not have preservatives.

—Select whole-wheat and whole grain breads which add fiber and complex carbohydrates to your lunch.

—Toast the bread to keep it fresh and firm. This works well when you are preparing your lunch in advance as well.

—Do not butter the toast.

—These sandwiches are open-faced to give you half the calories of a two-slice sandwich, but there is no reason you can't "put a lid on it" if you prefer a closed sandwich.

—Most of the recipes here are designed to make four sandwiches.

—Many of the recipes recommend Gouda cheese, it being a European favorite. Any other cheese may be substituted, to suit the tastes of the family.

RAISIN TOAST

4 tbsp. raisins	pinch of marjoram
6 tbsps. red wine	2 sour apples
4 slices bread	4 slices Gouda cheese
¼ lb. liver veal sausage	

Wash the raisins and add to the red wine. Bring to a boil and let simmer for 20 minutes. Toast the bread, spread with the liver sausage and sprinkle with a dash of marjoram. Peel the apples, remove the core and slice into ¼ inch thick rings. Lay an apple ring on each slice of toast, top with a slice of Gouda, and brown in a preheated oven, until the cheese melts.

TOASTED BOMBAY SANDWICHES

4 slices bread	2 medium onions
butter for toasting	2 bananas
1 package fish sticks (10)	curry
dash of ginger	4 slices Gouda cheese
juice from ½ lemon	
4 tbsp. grated coconut	

In a frying pan, brown the bread slices on one side until golden yellow; remove. Heat fish sticks. Meanwhile, saute the half-moon cut onions; add the banana slices and braise together briefly. Season with the spices and lemon juice, and fold in the grated coconut. Portion the banana-onion mixture on the toasted side of the bread, lay the fish sticks on top and cover each with a slice of Gouda cheese. Fry the untoasted side of the bread in butter on low heat for 9–10 minutes. The toast can be served when the cheese begins to melt.

TUNA TOAST

1 7 oz. can tuna fish	1 tbsp. mayonnaise
1 large onion	4 slices bread
1 tbsp. capers	1 orange
pepper	½ cup grated Gouda

Drain the tuna. With 2 forks, toss the tuna as if you were tossing a salad. Dice the onions, chop the capers and blend all ingredients with pepper and mayonnaise. Toast the bread and portion the mixture evenly on top. Peel the orange with a sharp kitchen knife, not leaving any of the white skin on the orange. Cut into slices and lay on the bread. Sprinkle with Gouda and bake the toast in a pre-heated oven at 350 degrees for 5–8 minutes.

SPINACH TOAST

1 lb. fresh spinach	2 hard-boiled eggs
2 tbsps. butter	pepper
1 onion	4 slices Gouda cheese
salt	4 slices bread
nutmeg	

Wash spinach. Steam until leaves are loose and drain on a sieve. Heat butter, saute the diced onions until glazed, and briefly toss in the spinach. Season to taste with salt and nutmeg. Toast the bread, let it cool, spread lightly with butter on one side, and top with spinach. Slice the eggs and lay over the spinach. Lightly pepper and top each toast off with a slice of Gouda cheese. Brown in pre-heated oven or under a broiler, until the cheese begins to melt.

APPLE-TOMATO TOAST

4 slices bread	salt, pepper, marjoram
1 large apple	4 slices Gouda cheese
3 large tomatoes	

Pre-toast the bread. Peel the apple and cut into fourths. Remove the core and cut into ¼ inch thick slices; the tomatoes likewise. Overlay the toast with apples and tomatoes, season and top it off with a slice of cheese. For best results, to ensure that the apples and tomatoes will be hot enough, bake in a pre-heated oven at 350 degrees for 5 minutes, until the cheese begins to melt.

OPEN-FACE STEAK SANDWICHES

4 slices bread, crust removed	1 bunch parsley
8 tbsp. butter	small glass cognac/brandy
4 filet steaks (4 oz. each)	4 slices Gouda cheese
salt	
coarse black pepper	

In the frying pan brown both sides of bread in about 3 tbsp. butter. Remove, and set on a pre-warmed plate. Add the remaining butter in the pan. Run both sides of the steak in pepper and fry each side for 3 minutes. Lightly salt, and set on the bread. Add the finely-chopped parsley into the frying-pan drippings, quench with cognac and pour over the steaks. Top with a slice of Gouda cheese and place under pre-heated broiler for 2 minutes.

SPICY ONION SANDWICHES

8 slices bread	dash of caraway seed
4 tbsp. mayonnaise	⅔ cup aged Gouda cheese
10 medium onions	

Remove the crusts from the bread. Spread lightly with mayonnaise and cut diagonally. Remove the onion skins, cut into very thin half-moon shapes, and lay on the bread. Top with the remaining mayonnaise, sprinkle with caraway seeds to taste and sprinkle heavily with grated Gouda cheese. Set the bread on a cookie sheet and bake until golden yellow in a pre-heated oven at 350 degrees for 8–10 minutes.

DEDDIE'S SPECIAL

4 slices toast	salt and pepper
1 tbsp. butter	4 oz. sour cream
5 oz. mushrooms	tabasco sauce
lemon juice	parsley
rosemary	2 oz. grated cheese
thyme	

Spread the slices of toast with butter. Wash and slice the mushrooms, sprinkle with a little lemon juice and saute for a few minutes, together with the herbs, in the hot butter. Stir in the sour cream, tabasco sauce and chopped parsley and spoon over the toast. Top with grated cheese and grill until the cheese melts and begins to bubble.

CLUB SANDWICH

3 slices wheat bread	mustard
3 slices rye bread	1 slice ham
lettuce leaves	cucumber
1 slice American cheese	1 oz. blue cheese
1 tomato	2 strips Swiss cheese
3 slices bacon	2 grapes
1 slice Gouda cheese	red pepper

Layer a slice of wheat bread with lettuce leaves and a slice of American cheese, then a slice of rye bread with sliced tomato and crisply fried bacon, a slice of wheat bread with a slice of Gouda cheese spread with a little mustard and a slice of rye bread with ham and slices of cucumber. Cover with a slice of wheat, spread with blue cheese, butter and topped with a lettuce leaf. Lastly, put on a slice of rye and a slice or two of Swiss cheese, garnished with grape halves and strips of red pepper. Let guests choose the layer that suits each individual taste.

HAM AND SAUERKRAUT TOAST

4 slices bread	4 slices pineapple
4 slices ham	½ cup grapes
1 cup sauerkraut	4 slices aged Gouda
3 onions	

Toast the bread on one side, and lay a slice of ham on the untoasted side. Cut the onions into small cubes and pineapple into strips, and combine them together with the halved grapes and the sauerkraut. Pile the mixture on the toast and top it off with a slice of Gouda cheese. Brown under the broiler until the cheese begins to melt.

ENGLISH RED HERRING TOAST

2 large red herring or	2 hard-boiled eggs
1 smoked mackerel	dash of pepper
4 slices toast	½ cup aged Gouda cheese

Bone the herring or mackerel, skin and portion evenly on the toast. Slice the hard-boiled, peeled eggs, lay them on the toast and season with fresh pepper. Sprinkle heavily with grated mature Gouda cheese and bake in pre-heated oven at 400 degrees for 5–8 minutes. Under the broiler it takes 2–3 minutes to brown; check oven often.

CORNED BEEF TOAST

4 slices bread	2 medium dill pickles
2 tbsp. butter for spreading	½ bunch chives
4 thick slices corned beef	4 slices aged Gouda
3 hard-boiled eggs	

Toast the bread, let it cool, and spread lightly with butter. Lay the corned beef over the toast. Slice the eggs and dill pickles, distribute onto the toast and sprinkle with chopped chives. Cover each toast with a slice of Gouda cheese and brown in a pre-heated oven or under a broiler.

GROUND BEEF TOAST

4 slices bread	2 egg yolks
ketchup	1 tsp. paprika
1 cup lean ground beef	salt, pepper
1 diced onion	½ tsp. mustard
4 slices Gouda cheese	

Brown the toast on one side until golden yellow, and spread this side lightly with ketchup. Work the beef, onion, egg yolks and seasoning to spicy meat dough and portion evenly on the toast with ketchup. With the meat side down, cook for 4–5 minutes in the frying pan. Flip over, top each toast with a slice of Gouda cheese, and fry on low heat, covered, until the cheese is melted.

SANDWICHES FOR ONE

*All ingredients in this section are for preparation of
one sandwich.*

TOASTED CHEESE AND
CHICKEN SANDWICH

2 slices whole wheat bread	4 radishes
1 oz. grated Edam cheese	salt and pepper
1–2 oz. cooked chicken	

Sprinkle half of the grated cheese on one of the slices
of toast, arrange the pieces of cooked chicken on top,
cover with chopped radishes, sprinkle with a little salt
and pepper and the rest of the grated cheese. Heat under broiler and then place the other slice of bread on
top, if desired.

TOASTED CHEESE AND
MUSHROOM SANDWICH

1 oz. fresh mushrooms	salt and pepper
pat of butter	seasoned salt
2 slices whole wheat bread	2 green pepper rings
2 slices Gouda cheese	

Saute the mushrooms in butter. Put a slice of cheese
onto one of the slices of bread and arrange the
mushrooms on top. Season with a little salt, pepper
and seasoned salt, then cover with the rings of pepper
and the second slice of cheese. Heat under broiler until
cheese melts and then top with the second slice of
bread.

TOASTED CHEESE AND BANANA SANDWICH

2 slices whole wheat bread	1 tbsp. raisins or honey
2 slices Gouda cheese	pat of butter
½ banana	

Cover one piece of bread with a slice of cheese topped with sliced banana and garnish with raisins or honey, to taste. Complete the sandwich with the second slice of cheese and bread. Butter the outer side and grill in a frying pan as you would a grilled cheese sandwich.

GOURMET TOAST

1 slice white toast	1 slice mature Gouda
pat of butter	fine chopped parsley or
2 slices bacon	ground paprika
2 slices tomato	

Butter the toast. Cover with layers of bacon, sliced tomato and lastly with the slices of cheese. Place on the top shelf of an oven pre-heated to 450 degrees for 10 minutes or under the grill until the cheese melts and turns golden brown. Sprinkle with finely chopped parsley or paprika powder.

TOASTED CHEESE AND FISH SANDWICH

1 fish fillet	1 slice mature Edam cheese
large pat of butter	parsley
2 slices bread	lemon juice

Fry the fish stick in the butter until cooked through. Put a slice of cheese onto one of the slices of bread and cover with the fish stick. Sprinkle generously with chopped parsley and a few drops of lemon juice. Top with the other slice of bread.

TOASTED CHEESE AND HAM SANDWICH

pat of butter	1 slice ham
2 slices bread	2 slices young Gouda

Butter the slices of bread. Cover with ham slices between the two slices of cheese and top with the second slice of bread. Butter the outside of the sandwich and toast in a frying pan.

LOW-CAL SANDWICH

2 slices whole wheat bread	2 tbsps. chopped celery
or 2 slices rye	½ green pepper
2 slices light American cheese	salt

Put a slice of cheese onto one of the slices of bread. Arrange the chopped celery and the pepper rings on top; sprinkle with a little salt. Cover with the other piece of cheese and broil or add the second slice of bread and fry.

QUICK PIZZA

1 slice Italian bread	garlic powder
pat of butter	2 anchovy fillets
1 tomato	cocktail onions
pepper	1 slice aged Gouda
oregano	finely chopped parsley

Butter the toast. Slice the tomato and arrange on top of the toast. Sprinkle lightly with pepper, oregano and garlic powder. Garnish with the anchovies and cocktail onions. Arrange strips of cheese in a lattice pattern on top so that the anchovies can still partly be seen. Place on the top rack of an oven pre-heated to 450 degrees for 10 minutes or under the grill until the cheese melts and turns golden brown. Sprinkle with finely chopped parsley. (Mushrooms, pepperoni or other toppings may be substituted for anchovies.)

TOAST WILLIAMS

1 slice whole wheat bread	1 slice Gouda cheese
1 tsp. mayonnaise	finely chopped parsley
1 slice ham	ground paprika
½ pear (canned)	

Spread the mayonnaise on the toast. Cover with the ham and put the well-drained pear half on top with the slice of cheese on top of the pear. Place on the upper shelf of an oven pre-heated to 450 degrees for 10 minutes or under the grill until the cheese melts and becomes golden brown. Garnish with parsley and ground paprika.

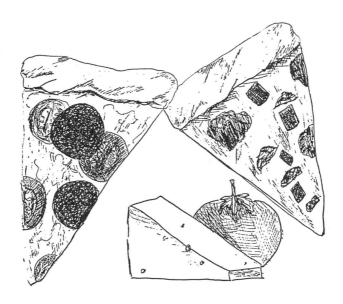

PIZZA TIPS

—All the ingredients for the dough are found in the individual recipes; the directions are fully explained under "Pizza Neapolitan."

—You can prepare large or small, round or square pizzas. The diameter of a normal pie is 20″.

—Pizza can be made ahead, then frozen and placed in the microwave for a fresh, hot lunch or snack.

—Once again, while the European preference is Gouda cheese, you may substitute mozzarella, cheddar or whatever cheese suits your pizza palate.

NEAPOLITAN PIZZA

Dough:	Topping:
1½ lbs. flour	butter for spreading
2 tbsp. yeast	¼ cup grated Gouda cheese
1 tsp. sugar	2 lbs. tomatoes
1 cup milk	black pepper
1 egg	pinch of garlic salt
pinch of salt	oregano
	½ cup sliced salami
	1 cup aged Gouda

Dough Directions for All Pizzas
Sift the flour into a bowl. Form a hole in the middle and crumble the yeast into it. Sprinkle with sugar and add a tbsp. of the lukewarm milk. Sprinkle the chunk of yeast with flour. Cover the bowl with a towel and set in a warm place. A 125 degree oven works well, leaving the door ajar. After 15 minutes you will see cracks in the flour; the chunk of yeast has disappeared. Dissolve the butter in the warm milk and blend with the egg and salt into the dough. Then beat vigorously until the dough has doubled in size.

Four Individual Neopolitan Pizzas
Meanwhile grate the mature Gouda cheese; wash the tomatoes, cut into slices, and shred the middle-aged Gouda cheese into coarse shavings with the grater. Knead the risen dough, form into a roll, cut into 4 equal, large pieces, each about 7 oz. Shape into balls and roll them out with a rolling pin until they are about 6 inches round. Lay 2 crusts on a greased cookie sheet, and 2 on a grid covered with aluminum foil. Put all 4 crusts into the oven at once, close the oven door, and let rise for 8 minutes. Then heat the oven to 375 de-

grees and pre-bake for 15 minutes. Remove both cookie sheets. Dab the pies with butter, sprinkle with the mature Gouda cheese, top with tomato slices, season, place the salami slices in the open spaces and sprinkle heavily with the coarsely grated Gouda cheese. Bake for 10 minutes more; halfway through remove the cookie sheets. Serve hot.

ONION-BACON PIZZA

Dough:	Toppings:
1 heaping cup flour	6 tbsps. ketchup
1 tbsp. yeast	1 cup onions
½ tsp. sugar	¼ cup lean bacon
½ cup milk	black pepper
2 tbsps. butter	1¾ cup aged Gouda
½ egg (Beat an entire egg, and use half for dough).	
dash of salt	

Prepare the dough from the above ingredients in the same manner as for the Neapolitan Pizza. While the dough is rising, cut the onions and bacon into cubes; combine both ingredients. Coarsely grate the Gouda cheese. As soon as the dough has doubled in size, knead through once, roll out to a round pie to fit the pizza pan, mold it into the greased pan, and spread with ketchup. Pour over the onion-bacon mixture and season vigorously with fresh pepper. Bake the pizza in a pre-heated oven at 350–375 degrees for 20 minutes, until golden brown. Briefly remove the pan, sprinkle heavily with grated cheese and bake further for 5 minutes.

SPICY GROUND BEEF PIZZA

Dough:	Toppings:
1 heaping cup flour	¼ cup butter
1 tbsp. yeast	2 onions
½ tsp. sugar	1 green pepper
½ cup milk	¾ lb. lean ground beef
2 tbsp. butter	1 tsp. paprika
½ egg (beat entire egg and	dash of salt
use half for dough)	tbsp. ketchup
dash of salt	1¾ cup grated Gouda

Prepare the dough from the above ingredients as for Neapolitan Pizza. While the dough is rising, saute the diced onions in hot butter. Wash the green pepper and cut into narrow strips. Braise with the onions for 5 minutes, then add the meat. Braise everything for 3–4 minutes. Season with the spices and ketchup. Coarsely grate the Gouda cheese. After the dough has doubled in size, knead through once, roll out to a round pie to fit the pizza pan. Set the dough on the greased pan and mold into place. Spread the cooled mixture on top, and bake the pizza until golden brown in a pre-heated oven at 350–375 degrees for 20 minutes. Remove the pan, sprinkle the pizza heavily with grated cheese and bake for 20 minutes.

"THE POOR KNIGHT"
(Quick Pizza)

Toppings:	"The Poor Knight"
2 tbsp. butter	1 cup milk
¼ cup bacon	3 eggs
2 onions	dash salt
6 skinned tomatoes	pepper
dash marjoram	8 slices Italian bread
dash thyme	butter for frying
black pepper	
⅔ cup Gouda cheese	
1 bunch parsley	

In hot butter, fry the bacon and onions until glazed. Skin the boiled tomatoes, cut into eighths and stew with the bacon and seasonings. (Canned, stewed tomatoes save time here.) Cut the Gouda cheese into ½ inch cubes and add them together with the chopped parsley. Keep the mixture on low heat.

Combine the milk, eggs, and spices and whisk until smooth. Pour onto a plate and soak the bread slices well on both sides. In a frying pan, heat the butter and fry the bread slices on both sides until golden brown. Top with the tomato mixture and serve.

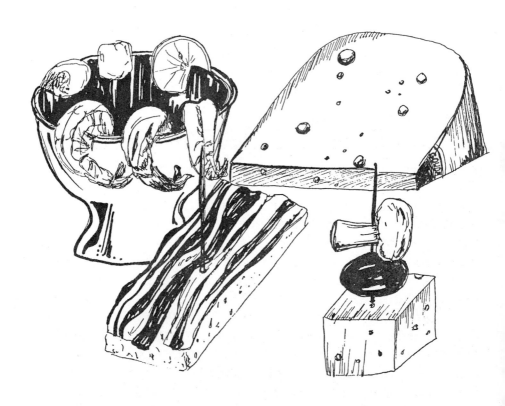

APPETIZERS, HORS D'OEUVRES, FONDUES AND DIPS

Finger foods are fun foods. They can be an appetite stimulant before a meal or they can be a meal in themselves. An easy evening for a hostess can consist of setting a table with hot and cold hors d'oeuvres and appetizers, a selections of dips, meat, cheese and fruit fondues and letting guests help themselves.

Appetizer Tips

—Prepare cold delicacies in advance and refrigerate.

—Prepare everything in bite-sized portions and concentrate on finger foods, which make clean-up easier.

—Several fondue pots can provide an interesting selection. It might work best to use pots that burn Sterno or alcohol to eliminate the need for electrical outlets.

—For color, garnish platters with parsley, tomato wedges, lettuce leaves and other edible garnishes.

APPETIZERS AND HORS D'OEUVRES

GOURMET MINI SAUSAGES

4 mini sausages	1 slice Gouda cheese
mustard	½ inch thick
ketchup	4 strips bacon
paprika	vegetable oil

Cut the sausages lengthwise, and leave ½ inch on each end uncut. Spread the mustard and ketchup on each flat side of the sausages, and sprinkle lightly with paprika. Remove the rinds from the cheese, cut into strips the width of your finger, and stuff into the sausages. Wrap each sausage with a bacon strip, hold in place with 2 toothpicks, daub lightly with vegetable oil and bake in a pre-heated oven, until the cheese begins to melt.

MINI ONION CRUSTS

10 oz. onions	2 tbsps. sour cream
dash of pepper	⅓ cup aged Gouda
3 tbsps. of flour	butter
3 eggs	

Peel the onions and dice finely. Lightly salt, pepper well. Dust with flour. Add eggs, cream and grated Gouda cheese and whip well. Heat the butter and with a teaspoon, spoon in small crusts into the pan. Fry until golden yellow.

MINI CHEESE NUTS

1 cup butter	½ tsp. worcestershire
1 cup aged Gouda	pepper
½ bunch parsley	1 cup walnuts
1 tsp. rum	

Whip the butter until foamy and add the grated cheese; season to taste with finely-chopped parsley and seasonings. With 2 teaspoons, form small clots from the cream. Set on aluminum foil and press 2 sides of the clots with walnut halves. Chill for at least 1 hour, until firm.

DUTCH HAM AND CHEESE BALLS

2 tbsps. mayonnaise	1 tsp. chopped caper
1 tbsp. mustard	2 hard-boiled eggs
⅓ cup Gouda cheese	1 bunch parsley
4 oz. cooked ham	

Whip the mayonnaise and mustard, and blend in the coarsely-grated Gouda cheese and ham, cut into very fine cubes, the chopped capers, and the eggs. Season to taste. Shape the mixture into small balls and roll them in chopped parsley. Use toothpicks for skewering.

HERB CHEESE SNACKS

cubes of herb, caraway or smoke cheese
pickles
mushrooms
cocktail onions
green olives

Cut the cheeses into medium-sized cubes. Garnish with a slice of pickle, a slice of mushroom and a cocktail onion or green olive. Use toothpicks to skewer.

LOBSTER AND CREAM CHEESE PUFFS

3 pkgs. cream cheese
8 oz. concentrated cream of lobster soup
pastry shells

Remove cream cheese from the refrigerator and allow it to come to room temperature. Whisk the cream cheese into the lobster soup until smooth. Pipe or ladle the mixture into pastry shells.

OLIVE SNACKS

8 oz. grated aged cheese	pinch of salt
4 oz. butter	ground paprika
5 oz. flour	1 can olives

Knead the cheese, butter, flour and seasonings into a soft dough. Drain the olives well. Mold the dough into small balls, press an olive into the middle of each, making sure that it is well covered with dough. Put the balls onto a baking sheet and bake in a pre-heated oven at 450 degrees for about 15 minutes. Serve hot.

TOASTED CHEESE AND BACON FINGERS

1 pat butter
8 slices bread
4 slices cheese
4 slices bacon

Butter four of the slices of bread, cover with a piece of cheese and an unbuttered slice of bread. Cut off the crusts and put them onto a baking sheet, together with the slices of bacon. Place the dish for 10 minutes in the top part of a pre-heated oven (450 degrees) until the cheese has melted and the bacon becomes crisp. Arrange the bacon on the sandwiches, slice into strips and secure with cocktail sticks. Serve hot.

STUFFED DATES

12 dates

1 package cream cheese

ground paprika

Cut the dates lengthwise and remove the stones. Allow the cream cheese to come to room temperature, then fill the dates with piped cheese. Garnish with ground paprika.

BACON ROLLS

10 strips young Gouda cheese

10 thin slices bacon

10 cocktail onions

Roll each strip of cheese in a slice of bacon. Garnish with a cocktail onion and secure with a cocktail stick.

HAM ROLLS

1 package cream cheese	seasoned salt
6 stuffed green olives	pepper
1 tbsp. fine chopped onions	ground paprika
and pickles	3 thin slices ham
2 tbsps. cream	

Allow the cream cheese to come to room temperature and mix with finely chopped olives, onions, pickles and cream. Season to taste with seasoning salt, pepper and ground paprika, then spread the mixture onto the sliced ham. Roll the ham up and refrigerate. Cut each roll into pieces 1 inch long and secure each with a cocktail stick. Makes 12.

FLORIDA COCKTAIL

1 egg white	ground paprika
lettuce leaves	seasoned salt
3 oz. crab (canned or fresh)	worcestershire sauce
1 grapefruit	pepper
2 tbsps. mayonnaise	½ tbsp. lemon juice
1 tbsp. tomato sauce	4 oz. sour cream
2 tbsps. sherry, madeira	parsley
or brandy	

For a festive garnish, first dip the rims of the glasses in unbeaten egg white and then in ground paprika. Put the lettuce leaves into the bottom of the glasses. Be sure that the crab is de-boned and arrange the pieces of crab and the sections of grapefruit (cut) attractively on the lettuce. Blend the mayonnaise, tomato sauce, sherry, madeira or brandy, seasonings and lemon juice until smooth, then stir in the sour cream. Pour the sauce over the cocktail and garnish with a sprig of parsley, ground paprika or a piece of lemon.

SHRIMP COCKTAIL

5 oz. shrimp	1½ oz. tomato sauce
1 egg white	2 tbsps. cognac
parsley	pinch of basil
lettuce	salt, pepper
1 cup coffee cream	1 lemon for garnishing
1 lemon	

Wash the shrimp and drain them well in a sieve. Garnish the rims of the glasses by dipping them in unbeaten egg white and then in very finely chopped parsley. Put a lettuce leaf into each glass. Divide the shrimp equally among the glasses. To make the sauce, mix the coffee cream adding the lemon juice drip by drip until the sauce has slightly thickened. Season with tomato sauce, cognac, basil, salt and pepper. Pour the sauce over the shrimp and garnish the glasses with a slice of lemon.

CHEESE MARBLES

5 oz. grated aged cheese	seasoned salt
⅓ cup breadcrumbs	ground paprika
2 eggs	finely chopped chives
pepper	fat for frying
salt	

Mix the grated cheese with the breadcrumbs, stir in the beaten egg and add the seasonings and herbs to taste. Mold into small marble-sized balls and fry golden brown in deep fat.

CHEESE FRITTERS

1 ½ oz. flour	1 egg
pat butter	5 tbsps. milk
1¼ oz. grated cheese	fat for frying

Make a batter with the flour, butter, cheese, egg and milk. Using a teaspoon, drop small amounts into the deep fat, which should not be too hot. Fry them for about 10 minutes until golden brown.

BANANA SURPRISE

2 bananas
3 thin slices ham
oil
4 tbsps. grated cheese

Peel the bananas. Cut them diagonally into three pieces and roll half a slice of ham around each piece. Secure with a cocktail stick, brush with oil and cover with grated cheese. Place under a pre-heated broiler until warm and golden brown in color.

CHEESE THUMBKINS

4 oz. butter	pepper
9 oz. flour	pinch of salt
3 egg yolks	6 oz. aged grated cheese

Cut the butter into the flour with two knives until it resembles coarse breadcrumbs. Add the remaining ingredients, knead into a soft dough and chill in the refrigerator for about 30 minutes. Shape into small balls, place on a buttered cookie sheet ½ inch apart. Indent the top with the thumb and bake in the middle of a pre-heated oven (375 degrees) for 15 minutes until crisp and golden brown.

CHEESE STICKS

Pastry:	Glaze:
3 oz. grated aged cheese	1 egg
6 oz. butter	1½ oz. grated cheese
1 egg yolk	
pinch of salt	
1 tsp. worcestershire sauce	
9 oz. flour	

Knead all the ingredients of the pastry into a smooth dough and chill in the refrigerator for 30 minutes. Roll out the dough thinly, brush the top with beaten egg and cover with grated cheese. Place the dough on a buttered baking sheet and bake in the middle of a pre-heated oven (375 degrees) for 15 minutes until crisp and golden brown. Cut at once into sticks.

SCALLOPED VEGETABLE PUFFS

4 pastry shells	pat of butter
6 oz. fresh vegetables	1½ oz. double cream
(peas, cauliflower, carrots, celery)	1 oz. aged cheese

Heat the patty shells. (Frozen pastry shells work well for this appetizer). Wash the vegetables, chop them finely and saute for 5 minutes in butter. Cool and then stir in the double cream. Fill the shells and cover with grated cheese. Place in the upper part of a pre-heated oven (450 degrees) or under a pre-heated grill until they turn golden brown.

CHEESE NIBLETS

Pastry:	Glaze:
3 oz. butter	1 egg white
3 oz. flour	1 oz. aged cheese
pinch of salt	½ tsp. ground paprika
1½ tbsp. water	
few drops of vinegar	

Cut the cold, hard butter into the flour and salt with two knives. Mix the cold water with the vinegar and knead it drop by drop into the pastry crumbs to make a dough. Chill for about 30 minutes in the refrigerator or for 10 minutes in the deep freeze. Roll out and fold, and re-roll into a rectangle 5 inches wide. Brush with loosely beaten egg white and cover with grated cheese mixed with the ground paprika. Press the cheese into the dough with a rolling pin. Cut into strips ¼ inch wide and twist into spiral shapes. Place on a baking sheet covered with aluminum foil. Bake in the middle of a pre-heated oven (425 degrees) for 12 minutes until crisp and golden brown.

JEWELS OF EDAM

3 oz. grated Edam cheese	mustard powder
2 tbsps. finely chopped parsley	2 tbsps. cream
celery salt	

Mix all the ingredients well, but keep a little chopped parsley for garnishing. Mold into marble-sized balls and roll these in the remaining chopped parsley. Refrigerate until firm.

BLUE CHEESE BALLS

3 oz. Blue cheese
1 oz. butter
20 walnut halves

Rub the Blue cheese through a sieve or blend in an electric mixer until creamy. Stir in the butter and chill in the refrigerator until stiff. With wet hands, mold into small balls and press half a walnut onto both sides.

CHEESE CROQUETTES

1 oz. butter	seasoned salt
1½ oz. flour	2 eggs
¾ cup milk	fat for frying
salt, pepper	breadcrumbs
6 oz. aged cheese	

Make a thick sauce with the butter, flour and milk. Remove from the heat and stir in the grated cheese. Add the seasonings if needed. Pour out over a wet dish and let it stand until cold. Using two spoons, form into croquettes. Coat with beaten egg and breadcrumbs, twice for a better finish and fry in deep fat until golden brown.

CHEESE TABLETS

4 oz. butter	celery salt
5 oz. grated aged cheese	pepper
5 oz. flour	2 drops worcestershire
2½ oz. milk	

Cream the butter, stir in 3 oz. of the cheese and add the sifted flour and milk alternately. Knead in the seasonings, roll the dough out into a large square and divide this into small square tablets. Place on a buttered baking sheet, allowing room for spreading and bake in the middle of a pre-heated oven (425 degrees) for 10 minutes until crisp and light golden brown. Cover with the rest of the grated cheese and bake at 175 degrees for a further 10 minutes until the cheese is golden.

FRIED CHEESE CUBES

6 day old white bread	¾ cup milk
1 egg	grated old cheese

Cut the bread into small cubes and dip them into beaten egg and milk. Coat with grated cheese, place on a buttered baking sheet and bake them in a hot oven until light brown.

HUNGARIAN BUTTONS

3 oz. self-raising flour	pinch of salt
4 tbsps. butter	½ tbsp. ground paprika
4 tbsps. (2½ oz.) grated aged cheese	pepper

Knead all ingredients together quickly and lightly. Shape into small balls and put onto a buttered baking sheet. Press flat with a wet fork. Bake them in the middle of a pre-heated oven (325 degrees) for about 20 minutes until crisp and golden brown.

FONDUES AND DIPS

—When preparing a cheese fondue, first rub the inside of the fondue pot with a garlic clove.

—Cheeses can be combined for unique flavors and can be thickened for dipping with a little corn starch.

—Breads that are ideal for cheese fonduing include Italian bread, hard rolls, French bread, brown bread and rye bread, cut into bite-sized pieces.

—Stir fondue cheeses both while they are melting and occasionally while they are warm and bubbling.

—Fruits and meats also make excellent dippers for fondue. Several recipes are suggested here.

—Sweet dips go well with cherries, mandarin oranges, apples, pears, bananas, walnuts, oranges, lychee nuts, butter cookies, pound cake and more.

—Fruits that turn brown when exposed to oxygen such as apples and bananas should be rubbed with lemon juice immediately after slicing.

—Spicy dips lend themselves to mini cocktail sausages, shrimp, mushrooms, Brussels sprouts, cauliflower florets, broccoli, chips and breads.

—Your own creative dips and dippers make the possibilities for fondue unlimited.

GOUDA FONDUE

1 clove garlic	white pepper
1 cup white wine	dash of nutmeg
2 cups Gouda cheese	4 oz. cherry brandy
1 tbsp. cornstarch	

Halve the garlic clove and rub it into the steel pot or fondue pot. Pour in the wine that was set out just before cooking. Coarsely grate the Gouda cheese, shake into the wine and stir constantly until the mixture is smooth. Combine the cornstarch with a little wine and blend into the fondue. Let it bubble, and season to taste with the seasonings. Finally, add the cherry brandy. Set the fondue pot on the burner, and let it lightly sizzle continuously while eating.

FONDUE THE BREWMASTER WAY

1 clove garlic	1 tbsp. cornstarch
4 tbsps. butter	dash of tabasco sauce
½ cup light beer	dash of worcestershire
½ cup malt beer	1 tsp. sharp mustard
2 cups Gouda cheese	1 tsp. ketchup

Halve the garlic clove and rub into the fondue pan on all sides. Add the butter, beer and coarsely-grated cheese. Heat up while constantly stirring, until the mixture is smooth. Combine the corn starch with a little beer, and blend into the mixture. Season the fondue with the spices, until hot. Set onto the burner and set out the bread, hard rolls or crackers.

APPLE WINE FONDUE

1 cup apple wine	1 tbsp. cornstarch
1 small onion	squirt of lemon juice
2 cups Gouda cheese	white pepper
¼ cup fresh mushrooms	1 tbsp. chopped dill
2 oz. raspberry spirits	

Pour the apple wine, along with the finely-diced onions, into the fondue pot; let it heat until bubbles start to rise, but do not boil, for 1–2 minutes. The onions should turn glazed. Coarsely grate the cheese and wash and slice the mushrooms into leaf-shapes and add both to the wine and stir. Just before boiling, the mixture should be smooth. Combine the corn starch with a little apple wine, and add to the fondue. Season to taste with the seasonings, dill and raspberry spirits. Set the fondue pot on the burner and "dunk" the bread into the fondue.

GOURMET'S SPECIAL FONDUE

2 tbsps. butter	pinch of nutmeg
½ clove garlic	white pepper
pinch of salt	4 egg yolks
2 cups cream	1 tsp. cornstarch
1½ cup grated Gouda cheese	4 oz. cherry brandy

Melt the butter in a heat-resistant pan or fondue pot. Coarsely chop the ½ garlic clove and rub lightly with salt. Let it sizzle in the butter for 1–2 minutes. Add 1½ cups of the cream with the coarsely grated Gouda cheese, stirring constantly. Add seasonings and slowly bring to a boil. Form a smooth mixture added with the remaining ½ cup cream, cornstarch and beaten egg yolks. Add the cherry brandy and serve. Do not let it sizzle any longer. You can re-heat this fondue without losing its good texture and flavor.

MUSHROOM FONDUE

5 oz. mushrooms	5 oz. young Gouda cheese
1 cup water	2½ oz. chopped ham
½ bouillon cube	pepper
1¼ oz. butter	salt
1¼ oz. flour	2 tbsps. chopped parsley
2½ oz. Swiss cheese	brown bread

Clean and slice the mushrooms, cook in the water (flavored with the bouillon) until tender. Melt the butter, stir in flour and very gradually add the mushroom broth until the sauce is thick and smooth. Cut the cheese into very small cubes, mix them into the sauce with the ham and heat until the cheese has melted. Add the mushrooms and season the fondue to taste with pepper, salt and finely chopped parsley. Dunk pieces of whole meal bread in the fondue or serve over slices of bread on a plate. This fondue is also excellent as a ragout.

FONDUE BOURGUIGNONNE

1 lb. lean sirloin
clarified butter
3 cups water
bouillon
2–3 tbsps. white wine
2–3 tbsps. soy sauce

Cut the meat into cubes. Heat the mixture in a fondue pot and fry the meat in the savory juices.

SWEET TOOTH FONDUE

½ cup milk	3 tbsps. honey
3 tbsps. butter	2 tbsps. cocoa powder
7 oz. semi-sweet chocolate	1 tbsp. cornstarch
¼ cup finely chopped,	2 tsps. Grand Marnier
roasted almonds	

Pour the milk into the fondue pot. Add butter and broken chocolate bar and dissolve while constantly stirring. Blend in the almonds, honey and cocoa powder. If necessary, thicken with cornstarch and season with Grand Marnier. You can dip lady fingers, pound cake and fruit in this mixture.

DIPS

Dips are spicy, cold, creamy sauces. Dips can be eaten with fruit, vegetables, chips or baked "dippers." You may also wish to serve wine, beer or juices with your dips.

FAMOUS DUTCH CHEESE DIP
(BASIC RECIPE)

5 oz. cream cheese
2 eggs
7 tbsps. fresh milk

Put cream cheese into the blender, add the eggs and the milk. After the mixture is blended smooth, pour into several small bowls and season with the various ingredients suggested below:

MUSTARD DIP

3 tbsps. Dutch cheese dip
2 tbsps. milk
1 heaping tsp. sharp mustard
1–2 drops tabasco sauce

HORSERADISH DIP

3 tbsps. Dutch cheese dip

2 tbsps. milk

2 tsps. grated horseradish

few drops lemon juice

few drops orange juice

ONION DIP

3 tbsps. Dutch cheese dip

2 tbsps. milk

1 small, finely diced onion

white pepper

APRICOT DIP

3—4 tbsps. Dutch cheese dip

2 tbsps. milk

dash of curry

1 tbsp. apricot preserves

TOMATO DIP

3 tbsps. Dutch cheese dip

1 tbsp. milk

2 small tomatoes, cut into fine cubes

black pepper

dash marjoram

SALMON DIP

1 small can salmon	seasoned salt
1 package cream cheese	ground paprika
capers	worcestershire sauce
coffee cream	tabasco sauce
salt	
pepper	

Break canned salmon into pieces with a fork. Blend the cream cheese with the liquid from the salmon, stir in the salmon and capers and add as much coffee cream as is required to make a thick sauce. Add the salt and seasonings to taste.

BACON DIP

8 slices of bacon	salt
2 tomatoes	pepper
⅛ cucumber	chives
4 oz. sour cream	

Fry the bacon until crisp and crumble it finely. Peel the tomatoes, cut into very small pieces and grate the peeled cucumber. Mix the bacon, tomato and cucumber with the sour cream and season to taste with salt, pepper and finely chopped chives.

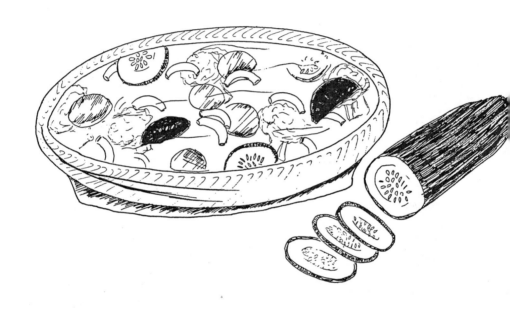

SOUPS

Soups can be served as an appetizer to a meal or as a meal itself, with hot, thick homemade bread. A meal of soup and bread is particularly appealing on cold winter nights. There may even be some scientific evidence to support the folk belief that chicken soup helps ease the symptoms of the common cold!

Soup Tips

—As a general rule, serve one cup of soup, if the soup is an appetizer, two if it is the main course.

—For people who don't have the time to simmer soup stock for hours, instant clear broth and instant clear beef stock works well as soup stock, as do bouillon cubes.

—If you do choose to make a homemade broth, make extra and freeze. Later, the broth can be thawed and vegetables and seasonings added.

HOT SOUPS

WESTPHALIAN THICK BEAN SOUP

2 tbsps. butter	1 package beans, frozen
½ tsp. flour	½ tsp. savory
1 quart broth	salt
½ cup aged Gouda cheese	

Melt the butter. Add flour and saute until golden yellow in color. Add broth, frozen beans, savory and a dash of salt. Simmer for 10 minutes, until the beans are fully cooked. Remove ½ of the beans with a skimmer and work the beans through a sieve. Finally round off the taste with grated Gouda cheese.

QUICK POTATO SOUP

1 tbsp. butter	¼–½ quart broth
2 packets instant potato soup	(instant or bouillon)
5 medium onions	⅔ cup aged Gouda cheese
5 oz. lean ground pork	1 bunch chives
1 tsp. paprika	
½ cup sauerkraut	

Saute the fine-diced onions in butter until glazed. Add pork and pull apart with 2 forks. Sprinkle paprika over pork and braise vigorously. Add chopped sauerkraut and stew 5–8 minutes. Prepare instant potato soup, add ingredients (meat or vegetables) and add 1 cup broth, until the right texture is achieved. Fold in cheese and chives.

COCONUT CREAM SOUP

½ coconut	1 egg yolk
1 cup milk	salt
1 can cream of chicken soup	curry
¼ cup aged Gouda cheese	4 tbsps. sweet whipped cream
a few strips of coconut	
with its brown outer coating	

Grate the coconut and pour boiled milk over it. Let it soak through for 5 minutes. Meanwhile prepare the soup according to directions. Fold in the coconut milk and the grated Gouda and thicken with the yolk. Season the soup to taste and pour into cups. Top each with a dollop of whipped cream and garnish with coconut strips.

FINE CHICKEN SOUP

1⅔ cans cream of chicken soup (11 oz.)	4 tbsps. condensed milk
	½ cup aged Gouda cheese
½ cup asparagus	½ tsp. curry
½ cup mushrooms	pinch of sugar
juice from ½ lemon	

Prepare cream of chicken soup according to directions. Add sliced asparagus and mushroom slices. Let the soup boil up once, fold in the condensed milk and grated mature Gouda cheese, and season the soup with curry and a pinch of sugar.

SHRIMP SOUP

⅓ lb. frozen shrimp	½ cup aged Gouda cheese
dash lemon juice	4 tbsps. cream
4–5 drops tabasco sauce	1 egg yolk
1 small package instant	½ bunch parsley
mushroom soup	
3–4 tbsps. ketchup	

Season the shrimp with lemon juice and tabasco sauce. Cover and let it soak for ½ hour. Prepare the mushroom soup according to directions. Fold in the ketchup, add the shrimp and bring to a boil. Fold in the grated cheese whisked with egg yolk and cream. Serve with minced parsley.

GERMAN VEGETABLE SOUP

½ leek	thyme
3 oz. young carrots	2 tomatoes
½ pepper	1½ oz. cucumber
3 oz. cauliflower	parsley
3 cups stock (instant	3 oz. American cheese
or from bouillon cube)	
1 oz. macaroni	

Clean the vegetables, cut the leek, carrots, pepper and cauliflower into small pieces and wash well. Bring the stock to a boil, add the vegetables, macaroni and thyme and cook for 20 minutes until the vegetables are tender. Peel the tomatoes and cucumber, cut into small pieces and cook in the soup for several minutes. Add the chopped parsley at the end of the cooking time. Cut the cheese into small squares and divide them among four soup bowls. Pour the hot soup on top and serve at once.

LENTIL SOUP

3 oz. lentils	1½ oz. butter
2 bay leaves	1 leek
thyme	1½ oz. brown rice
parsley	3 oz. old cheese
8 oz. potatoes	salt
1 onion	pepper

Soak the lentils in plenty of water for 4 hours, add the herbs and water so that it makes a total amount of 2 quarts. Add the finely chopped potatoes, after one hour's cooking and cook the soup for another 30 minutes. Meanwhile, saute the finely chopped onion, slice the leeks into rings and add them to the onion; saute until golden brown. Put the rice in the pan with the vegetables and fry gently for a few minutes longer. Sieve the soup over a pan and rub the lentils and potatoes through the sieve. Simmer the soup over low heat until the rice is cooked (30 minutes). Stir in the grated cheese, add the finely chopped parsley, salt and pepper to taste, but do not cook any longer.

POTATO AND TOMATO AU GRATIN

2 lbs. potatoes	1 onion
1 pat butter	salt
1 cup cheese sauce	pepper
1 egg	1½ oz. aged cheese
1 lb. tomatoes	parsley

Peel the potatoes. Slice them thinly and put a layer in the bottom of a buttered oven-proof dish. Cover with half of the cheese sauce. Pour the beaten egg on top then add the slices of tomato, the finely chopped onion, salt, pepper and finally the rest of the potatoes. Pour the remaining cheese sauce over the top. Sprinkle with grated cheese and then bake in the middle of a pre-heated oven (325 degrees) for 30 minutes until golden brown cooked through. Sprinkle with finely chopped parsley.

CHEESE SOUP

1 oz. butter	2¼ oz. aged cheese
1 oz. flour	parsley
1½ pint vegetable stock	seasoned salt
1 onion	
3 oz. coffee cream	

Melt the butter, stir in the flour and blend well—add the stock little by little, stirring continuously. To make a smooth, creamy soup, add more stock only after the first addition has been absorbed by the butter and flour mixture. Stir the grated onion and the coffee cream into the soup, remove from the heat and add the grated cheese, finely chopped parsley and seasoned salt to taste.

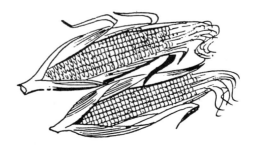

CORN CHEESE SOUP

1 onion	3 oz. cream
pinch of curry powder	salt, pepper
1 oz. butter	seasoned salt
1 oz. flour	1½ oz. grated cheese
1 pint bouillon stock	
small can sweet corn	

Saute the finely chopped onion and the curry powder in the butter. Add the flour, then gradually pour in the stock, stirring continuously. Mix in the contents of the can of sweet corn and cook for 10 minutes over low heat. Add the cream, salt, pepper and seasoned salt to taste. Remove from the heat and mix in the grated cheese.

SPINACH SOUP

3 tbsps. butter	10 oz. frozen spinach
1 medium onion	½ cup Gouda cheese
2 tbsps. flour	salt, pepper, nutmeg
1 quart with bouillon cubes	

Saute the diced onions in the melted butter until glazed. Add flour and brown until light yellow in color. Pour in the liquid and bring the soup to a boil; add the frozen spinach and let it thaw in the soup. Finally, blend in the grated Gouda cheese with a whisk; season to taste.

SPICY HERB SOUP

3 tbsps. butter	2 tbsps. each watercress,
3 tbsps. flour	parsley, chives
1 quart chicken broth (paste)	1 tbsp. each chervil,
½ cup Gouda cheese	tarragon, dill

Heat the butter and flour over low heat and add the chicken broth. Let the soup boil for a few minutes. Fold in the grated Gouda cheese, season with spices and finally add the chopped herbs and a pinch of garlic powder (optional).

CUCUMBER SOUP

1 cucumber	½ cup Gouda cheese
water	salt, pepper
1⅓ tbsps. butter	2 tbsps. dill
1⅓ tbsps. flour	2 tsps. chervil
1 cube bouillon	

Peel the cucumber from the outside to inside, cut in half, and scrape out the cores, if any, with a spoon. Dice the cucumber and puree in the blender. Keep adding water until the mixture equals 1 quart. Lightly heat the butter and flour, pour in the cucumber mixture, and let it cook thoroughly. Fold in the grated Gouda cheese and season with the spices and chopped herbs.

WINDSOR SOUP

6 oz. leg of veal	1 small onion
3 cups water	1 oz. flour
2 oz. macaroni	1 tbsp. madeira
1 oz. butter	1½ oz. cream
	salt

Put the cubed veal into boiling water, add a little salt and boil gently to make a strong meat stock. Cook the macaroni in some of this meat stock. Melt the butter and saute the finely chopped onion in it for about 5 minutes. Add the flour, stirring continuously and cook gently until it starts to brown a little. Gradually add the rest of the stock. Season the soup with madeira, the cream and salt if necessary. Cut the meat into strips and the macaroni into small pieces and add to the soup.

JULISCHKA

1 tbsp. butter	1 oz. semolina
3 oz. lean meat	3 cups water with bouillon
½ green pepper	2½ oz. grated cheese
½ red pepper	salt
	paprika

Melt the butter, stir in the meat breaking it up thoroughly with a fork and cook until light brown. Wash the peppers, remove the white pith and the seeds from the inside, slice and add to the fried meat, together with semolina. Fry gently for 5 minutes. Pour in the stock and cook for 10 minutes until the pepper is soft. Remove from the heat, cover with grated cheese and season to taste with salt and ground paprika.

CLEAR ONION SOUP

12 oz. onions	2 slices white bread
2 cups stock	2 oz. cheese
4 tsps. mustard	

Slice the onions into rings, cook until soft in the stock and add mustard to taste. Pour the soup into oven-proof soup bowls, float half a slice of bread on top of each bowl of soup and cover with grated cheese. Place the soup bowls under a pre-heated grill and heat until the cheese has melted.

SPARTAN SOUP

1 lb. carrots	a few slices celery
8 oz. onions	6 oz. aged cheese
1½ oz. butter	salt
2 lbs. potatoes	pepper
stock made with 1 quart water	seasoning salt
and 1 tbsp. yeast extract	
2 cups milk	

Cut the carrots and onions finely and saute in butter for 10 minutes. Cut the potatoes into cubes, add them together with ½ quart of the stock, to the vegetables. Simmer gently for 30 minutes. Stir in the rest of the stock, the milk and the chopped celery greens. Continue to cook a little longer, then remove the pan from the heat and add the cheese, cut into small cubes. Add salt, pepper and seasoned salt to taste and serve with French bread.

BULGARIAN SOUP

2 large onions	6 oz. salami
1 oz. butter	salt
1½ lb. sauerkraut	ground paprika
1 oz. flour	garlic powder
1 quart stock (2 cubes)	juniper berries
6 oz. cooked meat	8 oz. yogurt

Saute the finely chopped onion in the butter with the well-cut, well-drained sauerkraut until soft. Stir in the flour and the stock, blending well. Cook the soup for 10 minutes over a low flame and then mix in the meat and salami cut into thin strips. Cook for a few more minutes, add to the salt and seasonings to taste. Spoon a little yogurt into each bowl and pour the soup on top. Serve with rye bread.

COLD SOUPS

ANDALUCIAN SOUP

3 large tomatoes	thyme
3 tbsps. tomato puree	oregano
3 cups stock from bouillon	½ cucumber
½ oz. semolina	4 oz. sour cream
salt, pepper	

Cut the washed tomatoes into quarters and cook them for about 5 minutes in a little water. Rub them through a sieve and add the tomato puree. Pour the stock over the tomatoes, bring to a boil, stirring all the time. Sprinkle in the semolina and cook for a further 10 minutes. Add salt and seasonings to taste. Cool the soup. Wash the cucumber (do not peel) and cut it in paper-thin slices or chop into very small cubes. Serve the soup ice cold in cups or bowls and garnish with the cucumber. Just before serving, add a little lightly beaten sour cream to every portion.

COLD CREAM SOUP

1 lb. pineapple	lemon balm
1 cup water	1 cup dry white wine
¾ oz. sugar	½ cup double cream
⅓ oz. sago	

Clean the fruit, remove the seeds and cut the fruit into small cubes. Put aside the attractive pieces of fruit to use as a garnish. Cook the rest in the water and sugar for about 10 minutes. Puree in an electric mixer. Mix the sago with a little water, thicken the soup with it and add the lemon balm. Cook for 5 more minutes (stirring constantly). Cool the soup and when it is cold, stir in the wine and double cream. Serve ice cold, garnished with the fruit reserved for this purpose.

COLD BEET SOUP (BORSCHT)

6 oz. beef shank	1 onion
3 cups water	1 tsp. cumin seeds
1 bay leaf	1 potato
pinch thyme	grated lemon peel
salt	sugar to taste
few slices carrot	1 cup yogurt
celery greens	
12 oz. cooked beetroot	

Make a tasty stock with the shin of beef, water, bay leaf, thyme, salt, carrot and celery greens. Remove the meat. Peel the beetroot, grate it and chop the onion very finely. Sieve the stock, add the beetroot and onion and bring to a boil. Cut the meat into small pieces and add to the hot stock. Sprinkle the cumin seeds into the soup. Cook for about 30 minutes. Sieve the soup, bring back to a boil, grate the raw potato on top and cook until the soup has slightly thickened. Season with salt, grated lemon peel and a little sugar if desired. Cool and chill. Serve with a bowl of yogurt which should be spooned into the soup just before eating.

SALADS

Rich in fiber and fresh vegetables and fruits, naturally low in calories, the salad is the perfect addition to the meal and perfect as a meal by itself, especially when accompanied by a high-fiber bread. Salad before a meal can help to curb the appetite, particularly when accompanied by one or more large glasses of water.

Salad Tips

—Fresh lettuce wilts quickly. Rinse in cold water, then pat dry with paper towels or shake dry in a strainer to retain freshness.

—Fruits should be dipped in lemon juice before they are added to a salad. This will retard their tendency to turn brown in the air.

—Salads should be dressed immediately before serving.

—Salt should be used very sparingly on salads; it is not necessary to the flavor and can make salads containing cheese taste unnecessarily spicy.

—Always make the salad dressing or marinade before you make the salad. That way, the salad is fresher when served.

—Most of these salads can be made ahead, portioned into individual sealed plastic bowls, and taken to work as a light and healthy lunch.

SALAD VARIETIES

CALIFORNIA SALAD

1 cucumber	8 oz. sour cream
2 sharp apples	salt
1 orange	lemon extract
juice of 1 lemon	4 mint leaves
2 oz. raisins	celery salt
2 oz. walnuts	

Cut the cucumber, apples and peeled orange into small pieces. Sprinkle with lemon juice and mix well. Then add the soaked raisins and chopped walnuts. Stir a little salt and the seasonings into the sour cream and mix lightly into the salad.

NEAPOLITAN SALAD

3 tbsps. olive oil	3 oz. aged cheese
juice of 1 lemon	3 oz. ham
salt	3 oz. salami
pepper	1 large apple
2 shallots	1 small jar sweet gherkins
white part of 1 leek	lettuce leaves
½ tsp. crushed sage	

Make a dressing with the olive oil, lemon juice, salt, pepper, finely chopped shallots, finely sliced leek and crushed sage. Cut the rest of the ingredients, except for the lettuce into thin strips and mix with the dressing (reserve a little of the ingredients for a garnish).

Chill the salad for several hours, stirring once or twice. Serve on a bed of lettuce, garnish with the remaining ingredients, pickles cut into fan shapes and shallots.

CHICKEN SALAD

1 head celery	chives
1 red pepper	salt
1 cooked chicken	pepper
1 small can green beans	thyme
1 small can pineapple rings	3 tbsps. sherry
2 tbsps. mayonnaise	3 oz. raisins
4 oz. sour cream	lettuce leaves

Clean the celery, cut in strips, boil for five minutes in a little salted water and drain well. Remove the seeds and white pith from the pepper. Cut the pepper, chicken meat, green beans and pineapple into small pieces. Make a dressing with the mayonnaise, sour cream, chopped chives, salt, seasonings, sherry and soaked raisins. Pour this over the salad and mix well.

AMERICAN CHEESE SALAD

9 oz. aged cheese	4 tbsps. mayonnaise
1 red pepper	salt
2 large onions	celery salt
4 large sweet pickles	allspice
1 pound cooked potatoes	pepper
1 8-oz. can sweet corn	ground paprika
8 oz. sour cream	worcestershire sauce

Cut the cheese into tiny cubes, remove the seeds and white pith from the pepper and slice finely; chop the onions and pickles, slice the potatoes and drain the corn. Blend the sour cream, mayonnaise and seasonings and mix with the other ingredients. Taste and add more seasonings if necessary.

WINTER SALAD

1 large carrot	salt
1 cucumber	pepper
1 apple	seasoned salt
juice of ½ lemon	ground paprika
2 pieces endive	tabasco sauce
8 oz. yogurt	

Wash and grate the carrot, and mix with the cubed cucumber, chopped apple, lemon juice and the finely sliced endive. Stir the salt and seasoning into the yogurt and mix into the vegetables.

CONFETTI SPAGHETTI

5 oz. spaghetti	salt
1 bouillon cube	pepper
4 oz. ham	tabasco
6 oz. aged cheese	seasoned salt
2 pineapple rings	ground paprika
2 green apples	juice of ½ lemon
1 banana	2 tbsps. salad oil
8 oz. cooked peas	Worcestershire sauce
9 oz. yogurt	parsley

Boil the spaghetti in plenty of boiling water, flavored with the bouillon cube, until soft. Drain in a colander and rinse with cold water. Cut the ham and cheese into strips, the pineapple and apples into pieces and the banana in slices. Cut the spaghetti in small pieces and mix with the peas and other ingredients. Make a piquant sauce by mixing the seasonings with the yogurt and then stir the sauce lightly through the spaghetti salad. Garnish the salad with finely chopped parsley.

RICE SALAD DE LUXE

4 oranges	Garnish:
¾ lb. cooked chicken	1 orange
4 cups dry cooked rice	chives
14 oz. yogurt	
curry powder	
salt	
sugar	
lemon juice	
lettuce	

Peel the oranges, cut the sections into pieces and remove any pips. Cut the meat into small cubes and mix into the rice, together with the orange pieces. Blend the yogurt with the curry, salt, sugar and lemon juice to taste and mix into the salad ingredients. Line a salad bowl with lettuce leaves, put the salad on top and garnish with sections of orange and finely chopped chives.

SALAD JULIENNE

1 large carrot	salt
1 stalk celery	pepper
3 oz. aged cheese	tabasco sauce
2 apples	worcestershire sauce
juice of 1 lemon	thyme
1 small can peas	ground paprika
oil	seasoned salt
vinegar	

Cut the carrot, celery and cheese into very fine strips. Chop the apple finely and sprinkle with lemon juice. Drain the peas, and mix with the other salad ingredients. Dress the salad with oil, vinegar, salt and seasonings. Press the salad firmly into a rice mold, turn out and garnish with strips of red pepper and slices of cucumber.

POTATO SALAD

Dressing:	Ingredients:
5 tbsps. mayonnaise	2 lbs. baked potatoes
2 tbsps. condensed milk	½ lb. sausage
½ tsp. salt	1 fresh red pepper
3 tbsps. wine vinegar	2 medium dill pickles
5 drops tabasco sauce	2 hard-boiled eggs
2 tsp. chopped capers	1 cup Edam cheese
1 medium onion	

Make the dressing with the above ingredients; finally add the chopped capers and diced onion. Peel the potatoes, and cut into thin slices. Cut the sausage, pepper and dill pickles into small cubes. Carefully blend all the ingredients with the dressing. Cut the eggs into eighths and the cheese into thin slices, and blend into the salad. Set aside for 1 hour. Season to taste and serve. The potatoes should be well-cooled when making this salad. For best results, prepare this salad a day in advance.

SMOKED FISH SALAD

Dressing:	Ingredients:
1 cup yogurt	1 lb. smoked fish
1 tbsp. vegetable oil	(herring, halibut, mackerel)
1 tbsp. lemon juice	1⅔ cup celery
½ tsp. sugar	2 medium apples
pinch of salt	3 large tomatoes
1 bunch chives	6 lettuce leaves
1 small onion	⅔ cup Gouda cheese

Whip the yogurt with the vegetable oil seasonings and thinly-sliced chives. Remove any skin or bones from the smoked fish and break into bite-sized pieces. Cube the celery, apples and tomatoes; cut the lettuce leaves into strips and the cheese into thin slices. Carefully toss all ingredients with the dressing. The salad can be served immediately.

TROPICAL SALAD "MAJA"

Dressing:	Ingredients:
1 cup yogurt	1 bunch celery
juice from 2 lemons	1 can pineapple chunks
1 level tsp. salt	1 can morel cherries
1 tsp. sugar	⅔ cup walnut kernels
	1 cup baby Gouda cheese

Empty yogurt into a bowl and season with the ingredients. Wash the celery, peel, grate and add immediately to the dressing. Drain the pineapple and cherries separately on the sieve. Should the pineapple chunks be extra large, cut once again along the grain. Coarsely chop the walnuts and cut the Gouda cheese into thin slices. Combine all ingredients, except the cherries, with the dressing. Serve the salad promptly and only then blend in the cherries.

CRUNCH SALAD

Dressing:	Ingredients:
½ cup cottage cheese	1 package shrimp
½ cup yogurt	(frozen, 4 oz.)
¼ cup grated aged	1 head lettuce
Gouda cheese	1 green pepper
1 tbsp. ketchup	½ fresh cucumber
¼ tsp. salt	½ small container watercress

Whip cottage cheese with yogurt and grated Gouda, and season with salt. Thaw the shrimp as directed. Wash the lettuce, tear the large leaves in half, and dry well. Cut the pepper in half diagonally, remove the pulp and white ribs, rinse and cut into thin rings; shred the unpeeled cucumber into thin slices. Cut off the watercress with the kitchen shears, wash quickly and carefully and let dry. Serve on salad plates. Top each portion with 2 tbsps. dressing and shrimp.

SUSIE'S SUMMER SALAD

Dressing:	Ingredients:
1 cup yogurt	12 oz. mixed pickles
2 tbsps. mayonnaise	3 tomatoes
salt, pepper	½ fresh cucumber
pinch of sugar	¾ lb. bologna
1 bunch chives	½ cup baby Gouda cheese

Combine yogurt with mayonnaise, seasonings and diced chives. Drain the mixed pickles and cut the large ones into smaller pieces. Slice the tomatoes into eighths, unpeeled cucumbers into slices, and the bologna and cheese into strips. Add the salad ingredients to the dressing and combine well. Set aside to let it soak through, and serve on lettuce leaves.

SUMMER CHICKEN SALAD

Dressing:	Ingredients:
3 heaping tbsps. cottage cheese	½ small roasted chicken
2 tbsps. mayonnaise	4 slices pineapple
2 tbsps. ketchup	1 large apple
3 tbsps. pineapple juice	½ cup celery
juice from 1 lemon	1 cup baby Gouda cheese
salt, curry	1 cup green grapes
2 squirts tabasco sauce	
pinch of sugar	

Prepare a spicy dressing from the above ingredients. Drain the corn and beans well on a sieve. Slice the tomatoes into quarters, remove the pulp, and then slice the tomatoes and the Edam cheese into strips. Slice the bananas in half lengthwise, then in half-moon slices. Add, along with the other ingredients, to the dressing and combine. Chill ½ hour, season to taste, and serve.

MEXICAN SALAD

Dressing:	Ingredients:
1 cup yogurt	2 cans corn (8 oz.)
2 tbsps. mayonnaise	1 can French cut green
2–3 tbsps. herb vinegar	beans (8 oz.)
1 tsp. sharp mustard	3 peeled tomatoes
salt, pepper	¾ cup Edam cheese
dash of ginger powder	2 bananas

Prepare a spicy dressing from the above ingredients. Drain the corn and beans well on a sieve. Slice the tomatoes into quarters, remove the pulp, and then slice the tomatoes and the Edam cheese into strips. Slice the bananas in half lengthwise, then in half-moon slices. Add, along with the other ingredients, to the dressing and combine. Chill ½ hour, season to taste, and serve.

EMPEROR'S VIENNA SALAD

Dressing:	
½ cup mayonnaise	2 bananas
3 tbsps. condensed milk	1 fresh green pepper
3 tbsps. ketchup	½ lb. boiled ham
juice from 1 lemon	1 cup middle-aged Gouda
pinch of salt	

Thin the mayonnaise with the condensed milk, and season with ketchup, lemon juice and salt. Peel the bananas, slice and add immediately to the dressing. Cut the pepper into fourths, remove the white ribs and pulp and wash. Cut the peppers, meat and cheese into small cubes, all the same size. Combine with the dressing.

SPICY RICE SALAD

	Dressing:
1 cup rice	
1 leek	5 tbsps. vegetable oil
1 cup baby peas	5 tbsps. herb vinegar
3 red peppers, canned	salt, pepper
3½ oz. middle-aged Gouda	pinch of sugar
	1 bunch parsley

Add rice to vigorously boiling saltwater and boil 12 minutes; shake onto a sieve, drain, and let dry well. (You may also use Minute Rice or any instant white rice). Wash the leek thoroughly and cut into narrow strips. Put into the boiling saltwater for 5–8 minutes and drain, along with the peas, onto a sieve. Cut the peppers into small cubes, and coarsely grate the cheese. Put into a bowl with the other ingredients. Prepare a marinade out of the vegetable oil, vinegar, pepper, sugar and the finely-chopped parsley. Pour over the ingredients and toss well. Let the salad stand ½ to 1 hour. Don't forget to season before serving.

SAUERKRAUT SALAD

1 large sour apple	4 oz. sour cream
lemon juice	salt
6 oz. sauerkraut	pepper
2 shallots	seasoned salt
2 rings of pineapple	tabasco sauce
1 tbsp. raisins	thyme

Chop the apple finely, sprinkle with lemon juice and add to the raw, finely shredded sauerkraut. Chop the shallots finely, cut the pineapple in small pieces, then mix the shallots, pineapple and soaked raisins into the sauerkraut. Beat the sour cream with a little salt and the seasonings. Toss through the salad ingredients.

HERRING SALAD

5 oz. aged cheese	5 oz. mayonnaise
4 eggs	parsley
2 sour herrings	chives
1 large pickle	

Chop the cheese, hard-boiled eggs, herrings and pickle finely. Mix the mayonnaise with the chopped parsley and finely-chopped chives. Use this sauce to dress the salad, and garnish with mayonnaise, fan-shaped gherkins and chives.

TUNA AND MACARONI SALAD

9 oz. macaroni	garlic powder
1 bouillon cube	1 onion
1 cup sour cream	3 tbsps. sherry
salt	2 cans tuna
tabasco sauce	1 small can tomato puree
ground paprika	1 tomato
aroma salt	parsley
pepper	
worcestershire sauce	

Cook the macaroni in plenty of boiling water flavored with a bouillon cube. Drain in a colander and rinse with cold water. Mix the sour cream with the salt, seasonings, grated onion and sherry. Cut the tuna in small pieces and remove any small bones. Stir in the macaroni, then dress the salad with the sauce, seasoned with the liquid from the fish and the tomato puree. Garnish the salad with sections of tomato and chopped parsley.

GREEN BEAN SALAD

11 oz. frozen green beans	Marinade:
dash savory	4 tbsps. vegetable oil
½ lb. beef or pork sausage	3 tbsps. vinegar
½ lb. middle-aged Gouda	2 tbsps. water
¾ lb. tomatoes	¼ tsp. salt
	pepper
	pinch of sugar
	1 small onion

Prepare the marinade by adding the vegetable oil, while constantly beating, into the vinegar and water mixture. Season with salt, pepper, sugar and diced onion. Cook the beans as directed, about 10 minutes, with the savory. Drain and cool on a sieve. Cut the sausage and cheese into strips, remove the pulp from the tomatoes and cut likewise. Pour the marinade over the prepared ingredients and set the salad aside for ½ hour.

COUNTRY SALAD

1–2 heads Boston lettuce	Dressing:
⅓ lb. thick-sliced ham	1 cup yogurt
½ cup middle-aged Gouda	½ container sour cream
2 hard-boiled eggs	2 tbsps. mustard
	dash of pepper

Wash the lettuce, cut through the entrecote. Tear the large leaves in half, rinse, dry well, and toss into a bowl. Cut the ham and cheese into small cubes, and the eggs into eighths. Pour the beaten dressing mixture over the ingredients and toss lightly. This salad should be served immediately.

DUTCH SALAD

Dressing:	Salad:
⅔ cup mayonnaise	½ cup middle-aged Gouda
3 tbsps. condensed milk	2 pickled herring
pinch of sugar	1 large dill pickle
1 bunch chives	2 tbsps. chopped onions
	4 hard-boiled eggs

Whip the mayonnaise with the condensed milk, until thinned. Season with a pinch of sugar and add the diced chives. Cut the cheese, herring and cucumbers into similar-sized cubes. Add the coarsely-chopped onions and the egg cut into eighths. Combine all the ingredients with the dressing. The salad should be set aside for an hour to allow the dressing to soak through.

CAULIFLOWER SALAD "EDAM"

1 medium cauliflower	Marinade:
juice from ½ lemon	4 tbsps. vegetable oil
1 small can baby peas	2—3 tbsps. vinegar
4 tomatoes	salt, pepper
1 cup Edam cheese	1 bunch parsley

Wash the cauliflower. With the head facing downward, lay in cold saltwater for 15 minutes. (Use 2 tbsps. salt for every 4 cups of water). Afterward set into boiling saltwater (1 tsp. salt for every 4 cups water) with the added lemon juice, and boil for 15 minutes. Remove the head with the skimmer, let it cook, and separate into rosettes. Thoroughly drain the peas on a sieve, and cut the tomatoes into eighths and the cheese into strips. Prepare the marinade dressing from vegetable oil, vinegar, seasonings and finely-chopped parsley, and pour it over the salad ingredients. Toss well but carefully and set aside for 15—30 minutes.

THICK BEAN SALAD

	Dressing:
1 package thick beans	½ cup smoked lean bacon
1 cup water	4 medium onions
pinch of salt	2 tbsps. vegetable oil
¼ tsp. savory	2 tbsps. vinegar
14 oz. can peeled tomatoes	fresh ground pepper
1 cup baby Gouda cheese	1 bunch parsley

Bring water to a boil. Add the unthawed beans with salt and savory and stew for 15 minutes, covered. Meanwhile cut the bacon into not-too-small cubes, and saute until glazed. Add the diced onions and saute until glazed. Add vegetable oil, vinegar and finely-chopped parsley to the bacon-onion mixture. Slice the cheese and add it to the mixture along with the warm beans and whole can of tomatoes with their juice. Combine carefully and let it set for ½ to 1 hour.

SAUERKRAUT SALAD "MANDARINO"

Dressing:	Salad:
1 cup yogurt	1 can mandarin oranges
1 tbsp. lemon juice	1 can sauerkraut
1 tbsp. mandarin juice	1 large apple
pinch of sugar	½ cup baby Gouda cheese
pinch of salt	

Prepare the dressing with yogurt and the mentioned ingredients. Lay the mandarins on a sieve and drain well. Chop the sauerkraut, if desired. Cut the apple into fourths, and then cut into thin slices. Cut the gouda also into thin slices, and toss the ingredients with the dressing. Season the salad to taste and serve immediately.

BRABANTINE SALAD

	Dressing:
2 heads Belgian lettuce	1 cup yogurt
1 tbsp. raisins	2 tbsps. honey
2 apples	½ tsp. sharp mustard
1 small can mandarin wedges	juice from 1 lemon
1 cup baby Gouda cheese	juice from ½ orange
	few lettuce leaves

Wash the Belgian lettuce. With a sharp knife, cut a thin slice and carve out the bitter pulp. Separate the sprays and cut into strips lengthwise. Simmer the raisins somewhat. Cut the pared or unpared apples into small slices. Combine the Belgian lettuce, apples, mandarins, raisins and Gouda cheese cut into strips. Prepare the dressing with yogurt and other ingredients, and pour over the salad ingredients. Chill for 15 minutes before serving and serve in a bowl garnished with lettuce leaves.

VEGETABLE SALAD "WESTLAND"

	Dressing:
1 can baby peas	Dressing:
1 can carrots	⅓ cup mayonnaise
1 can cut asparagus	3 tbsps. condensed milk
1 can cut mushrooms	salt, pepper
1 cup middle-aged Gouda	1 tsp. wine vinegar
	pinch of sugar
	1 small onion
	1 bunch parsley

Shake the vegetables into a sieve and drain well. Cut the Gouda into tiny cubes. For the dressing, thin the mayonnaise with condensed milk while beating. Season with the spices and blend in the diced onion and chopped parsley. Add the vegetables and cheese and toss with the other ingredients. Let the salad stand for 1 hour. Serve with toasted white bread.

HOMEMADE SALAD DRESSINGS

VINEGAR-OIL MARINADE

5—6 tbsps. vegetable oil	¼ tsp. salt
3 tbsps. vinegar	pepper
½ onion, if desired	pinch sugar

Pour the vegetable oil into a medium bowl. Combine with vinegar using a whisk. An emulsion develops. Dice onion into very small cubes, and add it to the mixture. Season to taste.

YOGURT DRESSING

1 cup yogurt	½ tsp. sugar
1 tbsp. vegetable oil	pinch of salt
1 tbsp. lemon juice	herbs (parsley, chives)

Whip the yogurt with the whisk until foamy. Add oil, seasonings and finely-chopped herbs. You can serve this dressing on a head salad and for all delicate light salads with fruit, vegetables or chicken.

HERB-MAYONNAISE DRESSING

¾ cup mayonnaise	2 tsps. capers
¾ cup dill pickles	1 tsp. mustard
2 onions	herbs (parsley, chives, watercress, dill)

Whip mayonnaise until smooth; if necessary thin with some water from the pickles. Dice the pickles, onions and caper. Combine with mustard and the chopped herbs. Ideal for potato and fish salad. Also great with fried fish and cold roast beef.

DOUBLE CREAM CHEESE DRESSING

2½ oz. double cream cheese	3—4 tbsps. milk
1 egg	2—3 tbsps. vinegar or lemon juice

Cut the double cream cheese into small cubes and beat with the egg, milk and vinegar or lemon juice until smooth. Enough for 3—4 salads and keeps in the refrigerator for a week. Tastes excellent with raw carrots, apples and cucumbers.

GOUDA CHEESE DRESSING

3½ oz. cottage cheese	¼ cup grated aged Gouda
½ cup ketchup	½ tsp. mustard
½ cup yogurt	¼ tsp. salt

Stir the cottage cheese with the yogurt until smooth. Add the grated Gouda cheese, mustard and salt. Season to taste. This dressing is great on endive salad, egg salad, mushroom salad, and also on cold beef.

MAIN COURSES

As we all know by now, the evidence shows that quantities of red meat can raise the blood pressure and the cholesterol level and block the flow of blood to the heart. The trick again is probably moderation. Refrain from eating red meat more than twice a week.

For that reason, we have concentrated our main course section on the savory meals that can be prepared using fish and chicken.

FISH

The meal which was once eaten by a large portion of the population on Fridays only has come into its own. Fish is now popular in soups and stews, fried, baked, broiled and even raw! Fish is no longer a coastal delicacy, and is much easier to work with due to commercial preparation.

—Rinse fish in cold water before cooking, then sprinkle with a few drops of lemon juice and let soak for 10 minutes. This firms the meat and reduces the fish smell.

—Salt fish before cooking. Salt extracts water from the fish.

—When buying commercially prepared fresh fish, ask for freshness dates and never buy fish that smells too "fishy."

—Melted butter, herb butter and lemon are the perfect accompaniments to broiled fish.

—Appliances and cookware which have been used to prepare fish should first be rinsed off with cold water after use, then washed in hot water.

FLOUNDER

4 fillets turbot or halibut	1 onion
(7–9 oz. each)	2 tbsps. capers
juice from 1 lemon	2 apples
salt	½ cup white wine
4 large tomatoes	4 tbsps. butter
¼ lb. thick slices ham	⅔ cup Gouda cheese
2 dill pickles	

Sprinkle the turbot or halibut with drops of lemon juice and salt. Boil the tomatoes, remove, slice and lay the fish in a large, greased, heat-resistant pan. Cube the ham, dill pickles and onion; chop the caper, divide the apple into wedges, and top the fish with all the ingredients. Pour over the wine and dot with butter. Cook thoroughly at 400 degrees for 20 minutes, then sprinkle the top with coarsely-grated Gouda cheese and briefly brown.

BROWN MULLET FILLET "BANANA"

2 lbs. mullet	8 tbsps. sweet, unwhipped
juice from 1 lemon	cream or condensed milk
salt	1 tbsp. ketchup
butter for greasing	½ cup aged Gouda cheese
6 tbsps. white wine	¼ cup almonds, slivered
2 small bananas	

Wash the red mullet, blot lightly with a paper towel. Rub the lemon juice and salt into the fillets, let soak through. Grease a heat-resistant pan well, place the fish into it and add wine. Crush the bananas, and blend with the cream, ketchup and grated, mature Gouda cheese. Finally, blend in the partially-roasted almonds. Spread the mixture evenly over the fish, and let it cook thoroughly at 400 degrees for 20 minutes. The top layer should have an appetizing color.

STUFFED TROUT

½ dry roll	2 hard-boiled eggs
4 large trout	½ bunch parsley
1 egg	white pepper
½ cup aged, grated Gouda	salt
1 4-oz. can mushrooms	butter for spreading

Soften the roll in cold water. Remove the fresh trout, then wash; thaw the frozen trout as directed, about 1 hour. Whip the egg with grated cheese. Cut the mushrooms into leaves, chop the egg, and blend with the chopped parsley, seasonings and the bread after the water has been squeezed out. Season the mixture to taste and stuff into the trout.

Now, you can make the trout in one of two ways:

—Lay each trout onto a sheet of greased tinfoil, wrap it up and set it on the greased pan or cookie sheet. Let it bake in the oven at 425 degrees for 15–20 minutes. The trout is served in the tin foil.

—Carefully place 2 toothpicks into the stomach. Melt the butter, brush it onto the trout and broil under a heated broiler for 5–6 minutes on each side. Serve with lemon wedges.

CODFISH FILLET IN EGG-CHEESE SAUCE

4 codfish fillets at 5 oz. each	1 large tomato
salt	2 hard-boiled eggs
juice from 1 lemon	½ bunch parsley
2 tbsps. butter	dash of salt
½ cup aged Gouda cheese	

Wash the fish fillets, blot dry, lightly salt and sour with lemon juice. Let soak through briefly and stew in the frying pan in butter until done—about 10 minutes. Keep warm on a hot plate. Pour the fish stock from the pan into a large measuring cup and keep adding the broth until it's 1 cup full. Saute the butter and flour in the frying pan until golden yellow in color. Add the broth and let it boil through once. Add the wine. Cut the Gouda cheese and tomatoes into small cubes, chop the boiled eggs, dice the parsley, and add all ingredients into the sauce. If necessary, salt to taste. Pour the sauce over the fish and serve with rice.

FISH SCHNITZEL "CAPRI"

7 oz. spaghetti	garlic salt
dash of salt	⅔ cup Gouda cheese
2 tbsps. butter	butter for frying
2 lbs. salmon fillet	1 can skinned tomatoes
juice from ½ lemon	(14 oz.)
⅓ cup flour	black pepper
1 egg	pinch of sugar
¼ cup breadcrumbs	
¼ cup Gouda cheese	

Simmer the spaghetti in 2 quarts of boiling water for 20 minutes and drain the water. Steam out until warm, swim the noodles in butter and put on a heat resistant plate. Keep in a warm place. While the noodles are boiling, wash the fish, blot dry with a towel, salt and sour with lemon juice. Let the lemon soak through briefly and run fish through a mixture of flour, broken egg and breadcrumb-cheese. Fry until golden brown on both sides in hot butter for 10 minutes. Set the skinned tomatoes in the pot or pan, bring to a boil, season to taste, and arrange over the spaghetti. Lay the fish fillet on top and serve together with a dish of grated Gouda cheese.

HALIBUT TOPPED WITH CREAM

4 cuts of halibut, 7 oz. each	4 tbsps. butter
salt	1 tbsp. flour
juice from 1 lemon	1 cup milk
4 large tomatoes	½ cup grated Gouda
butter for greasing the pan	dash of salt
	½ cup cream

Salt the halibut and cut the tomatoes cross-wise. Lay them on a greased, heat-resistant platter. Saute the butter and flour until golden brown. Add the milk, and let it boil through once. Blend in a grated mature Gouda cheese, and season to taste. Beat the cream until very heavy, and blend in the somewhat cooled sauce. Pour over the fish and tomatoes, set the latter into the oven, and bake the fish thoroughly, at 350 degrees for 20 minutes. The top of the cream should be golden brown in color.

FISH RISSOLE

2 lbs. salmon fillet	2 tbsps. breadcrumbs
juice from 1 lemon	1 egg
¼ cup water	1 small onion
¼ cup white wine	½ cup grated Gouda
¼ bay leaf	pinch nutmeg
5 peppercorns	butter for frying
1 small onion	

Wash the fillets, salt and sour with lemon juice. Vigorously boil the water, wine, seasonings and halved onions. Add the fish and let it stew thoroughly for 10–15 minutes. Remove the fish from the boiling water, let them cook, and crush coarsely with a fork. Work the breadcrumbs, egg, diced onion, grated mature Gouda cheese and nutmeg well into the fish. Let the entire mixture stand for a few minutes, so that it thickens, and then shape into 4 flat, round balls (rissoles). Cook in hot butter until crispy, golden-brown on each side, about 4 minutes.

FISH CASSEROLE

⅔ cup smoked bacon	salt
7 oz. onions	juice from ½ lemon
1 cup broth	11 oz. peeled tomatoes
1½ lb. potatoes	½ bay leaf
1 fresh cucumber	pepper
1½ lb. codfish fillet	⅔ cup baby Gouda

Cube the bacon, cut the onion into rings, and saute together until glazed. Add the broth. Add the following ingredients in layers: peel the potatoes and cucumbers, cut the potatoes into small cubes and the cucumbers in half. If desired, spoon out the pulp and cut the cucumbers into 1 inch sticks. Divide the salted and soured fish fillets into 2 inch cubes, and lay the whole tomatoes on top. Add the seasonings, boil up once, and simmer for 20 minutes. Then blend in the cubed Gouda, let melt and serve.

FISH STICK IN CURRY RICE

10½ oz. rice	2 bananas
1 tsp. salt	pinch cinnamon
12 cups water	juice for ½ lemon
3 tbsps. butter	½ cup Gouda cheese
1 tsp. curry powder	Egg Milk:
1 package fishsticks (8 sticks)	1 cup milk:
butter for frying and greasing	1 egg
1 jar morel cherries (9–11 oz.)	salt

Bring water and salt to a boil. Add rice and keep on boiling, uncovered, for 15 minutes. Drain the water and let the rice steam out. Heat the butter in the same pot, add curry, with a fork lightly toss the drained rice into it until well-covered, and let dry out slightly.

In a frying pan, cook the unthawed fish sticks in hot butter on both sides, until golden brown. Remove, keep warm and in the same pan, heat the pitted morel cherries, sliced bananas; season with lemon juice and cinnamon, and add the cubed cheese.

Grease a heat-resistant pan, pour in half the rice. Lay the fruit and cheese mixture and fishsticks on top and cover with half the rice. Beat the milk, egg and salt, and pour over the mixture. Bake for 20 minutes until golden yellow at 400 degrees.

FILLETS OF SOLE MARGUERY

8 sole fillets	4 oz. sour cream
8 wooden cocktail sticks	freshly ground pepper
2 cups water	thyme
1 bouillon cube	3 oz. peeled shrimp
For the Sauce:	parsley
1¼ oz. butter	lemon
1¼ oz. flour	
1½ cups fish stock	
3 oz. dry white wine	

Roll up the sole fillets and fasten them with cocktail sticks. Poach them in the water, flavored with a bouillon cube for 10 minutes. (Put the fish fillets into a shallow pan and see that the stock just covers them.) Melt the butter, stir in the flour, and add the fish stock and wine, stirring continuously. Do this over a low heat. Stir some of the hot sauce into the sour cream. Pour it back into the pan, stir and then add the seasonings and the shrimp. Remove the sticks from the sole fillets, arrange on a heated dish and pour the sauce over them. Garnish with a sprig of parsley and slices of lemon.

BRAISED HERRING IN TOMATO SAUCE

1½ cups coffee cream	marjoram
1 oz. flour	2 onions
1 small can of tomato puree	8 salt herrings
celery salt	3 oz. aged cheese
pepper	ground paprika
thyme	

Heat the coffee cream in a saucepan—blend the flour with a little of the cream and thicken the warm cream with this mixture. Stir in the tomato puree and add the seasonings to taste. Peel the onions and slice them into rings. Soak the herrings in milk for a few hours to remove some of the salt. Fillet the soaked herring and put the fillets into a buttered ovenproof dish. Cover with half the onion rings, cheese on top, make another layer with the onion rings, and top with the second half of the cheese slices. Put the dish into a pre-heated oven (400 degrees) for about 25 minutes until the cheese has melted and turned light golden brown. Sprinkle with ground paprika.

BANANA AND FISH AU GRATIN

2 bananas	Sauce:
1 pat butter	1¼ oz. butter
salt	1¼ oz. flour
3 oz. bacon	¾ cup milk
2 onions	¾ cup fish stock
	2½ oz. aged cheese
	2 tbsps. sherry

Peel the bananas, cut them in half lengthwise and fry quickly until golden brown. Cook the cleaned fish in salted water for 10 minutes, or until tender. Fill a buttered ovenproof dish with alternate layers of fish and banana. Fry the bacon slices in their own fat until crispy, remove from the pan. Cover the fish with bacon and onions. Make a smooth sauce with the butter, flour, milk, fish stock and three-quarters of the grated cheese. Stir in the sherry, and pour the sauce over the fish. Cover with the rest of the grated cheese. Place the dish on the upper shelf of a pre-heated oven (400 degrees) and bake for about 20 minutes until the crust is golden brown.

FILLETS BORDELAISE

salt	2 tbsps. white Bordeaux wine
9 oz. fish fillets	parsley
lemon juice	seasoned salt
4 slices young cheese	thyme
6 oz. mushrooms	oregano
1 onion	
2 tbsps. butter	

Salt the fish fillets, place on a piece of aluminum foil, sprinkle with lemon juice and cover with a slice of cheese. Saute the washed and quartered mushrooms and the finely-chopped onion in the butter. Add the wine, and stir in the salt and seasonings to taste. Spoon over the fish fillets and close the packets carefully. Bake the fish on the barbecue for about 20 minutes until tender.

FISH AU GRATIN

¾ lb. cooked fish	white wine
parsley	1½ oz. aged cheese
1½ cups white sauce, made with fish stock	2 tbsps. butter

Flake the fish and stir it into a white sauce made with fish stock, together with the chopped parsley. Flavor the ragout with a dash of white wine and spoon into a buttered oven-proof dish, cocotte dishes or ragout dishes. Cover with grated cheese—mixed with some breadcrumbs if wished—sprinkle melted butter on top and set the ragout in the upper part of a pre-heated oven (475 degrees) or under a hot grill until an attractive brown crust has formed.

COD PARCELS

1 pkg. frozen cod	1 green pepper
(¾ lb.)	3 oz. butter
curry powder	3 oz. shrimp
salt	
pepper	

Thaw the fish ahead of time and cut into four pieces. Rub them with curry powder, salt and pepper. Remove the seeds and white pith from the pepper and chop it finely. Cream and butter, stir in the shrimp and chopped pepper. Lay each piece of fish on a piece of aluminum foil so that the dull side of the foil is on the outside. Spoon the shrimp and butter over the pieces of fish. Close the packets carefully, with the join on the top and put them in a pre-heated oven (400 degrees) for 20–30 minutes. Serve with dry cooked rice.

FILLET OF FISH ON CELERY

2 large celery sticks	1 tbsp. flour
1 cup broth	½ cup sour cream
salt-pepper	½ cup aged grated Gouda
1½ lbs. red mullet or codfish	pinch thyme
juice from ½ lemon	pinch of sugar
2 tsps. butter	

Wash the celery sticks by brushing them, and boil with their rinds for about one hour; don't let them get too soft. Peel them, let them cool and cut into ½ inch thick slices. Season each side lightly, turn them in flour and fry in hot butter until light brown. Put them on a warm plate. Wash the fillets of fish, salt them, sprinkle with lemon juice, turn them in flour and fry in butter for 10 minutes. Lay them on the celery slices. For the sauce, heat the butter, saute the flour until yellow, and pour in the broth. Add the cream and the grated mature Gouda cheese and season to taste. Pour the sauce over the fish and serve with mashed potatoes.

FRIED FILLET OF FISH WITH CHEESE-REMOULADE SAUCE

Cheese Remoulade:	
2½ oz. cream cheese	4 fish fillets (5 oz. ea.)
1 egg	juice from ½ lemon
3—4 tbsps. milk	salt
2—3 tbsps. vinegar from dill pickles	pepper ½ cup flour
1 small onion	1 egg
2 dill pickles	¼ cup breadcrumbs
2 tbsps. capers	¼ cup grated Gouda
½ bunch parsley	butter for frying

Cube the cream cheese and put into a blender. Add the egg, milk and vinegar and blend until smooth. Add thinly-diced onion and dill pickles, as well as the chopped caper and parsley. Wash the fillets, blot dry well, rub with lemon juice, salt and pepper. Let soak through briefly. Take out 3 plates and fill one with flour, one with beaten egg and the other with a mixture of breadcrumbs and grated mature Gouda cheese. Heat the butter and fry the fillets, after coating them with the ingredients, on both sides for 8—10 minutes until golden brown. Serve the cheese remoulade sauce and boiled potatoes.

FRIED HERRING IN A CHEESE COATING

4 large herring	Sauce:
juice from ½ lemon	½ tbsp. butter
dash of salt	½ tbsp. flour
a few halved grapes	½ cup milk
½ cup young Gouda cheese	juice from ½ lemon
3 oz. flour	2 tbsps. sharp mustard
1 egg	dash of pepper
½ cup aged Gouda	
butter for frying	

Wash the herring. Sour with lemon juice; salt, stuff with grapes and Gouda cheese cut into strips. Close with toothpicks. Cover with breadcrumbs, and fry until golden brown on both sides. Grease a heat-resistant pan, and set herring into it. In another pan, saute the butter and flour, add milk, and season to taste. Pour the sauce over the herring and brown for 10 minutes at 400–425 degrees.

RED MULLET IN ALUMINUM FOIL

2 lbs. red mullet fillets	pinch of rosemary
juice from 1 lemon	3 peeled tomatoes
salt	½ cup young Gouda cheese
1 large onion	½ bunch parsley
½ cup lean smoked bacon	butter for greasing

Wash the fish, blot dry with a paper towel. Sprinkle with drops of lemon juice and lightly salt. Let soak through. Chop the onions, and cut the bacon into thin cubes, tomatoes into slices. Butter the tin foil, arrange a layer of fish over it, cover with the bacon and onion cubes, and season with rosemary. Top with the tomato slices, and place the cheese slices over the tomatoes. Cover with the remaining fish fillets. Cover the dish tightly with tinfoil, set in gas oven and bake at 375–400 degrees for 20–30 minutes. Serve sprinkled with chopped parsley.

FLORENTINE FISH RINGS

3 tbsps. butter	pepper
1 pkg. frozen spinach (10 oz.)	juice from 1 lemon
¾ tbsp. water	1 pkg. mashed potatoes
salt	(4 servings)
nutmeg	1½ lbs. tomatoes
1 pkg. frozen codfish	oregano
fillets (16 oz.)	⅔ cup aged Gouda cheese

Heat the butter and add the frozen spinach. Add water and thaw on low heat; season with a dash of salt and nutmeg. Partially thaw the codfish fillets, separate from each other, lightly salt, pepper, sour with lemon and cut into 2-inch wide strips. Prepare the mashed potatoes as directed, pour into a buttered casserole dish, and spread smoothly and evenly. Boil the tomatoes, remove, cut into slices. Divide the cheese slices into 2-inch squares. Sprinkle the fish and tomatoes with a dash of oregano; place the cheese at the inside edges of the pan in a criss-cross manner, and add the seasoned spinach in the center. Bake at 350–400 degrees for 30 minutes. Set the oven rack in the center of the oven.

CHICKEN

Naturally low in both calories and fat, chicken has become the preferred main dish of millions, replacing the red meat of the traditional meat-and-potatoes meal. Here, we offer some non-traditional European ways to fix chicken.

—Cook chicken by broiling or baking. Avoid frying when at all possible.

—No matter how you cook your chicken, remove the skin before eating, as calories and fat are present in very high quantities in chicken skin.

CHICKEN BREAST WITH MUSHROOM SAUCE

½ cup Gouda cheese	1 tbsp. capers
11 oz. fresh mushrooms	½ cup white wine
juice from ½ lemon	½ cup cream or condensed milk
4 tbsps. butter	1 tsp. cornstarch
4 chicken breast fillets	salt
2 medium onions	1 bunch parsley

Grate the Gouda cheese coarsely. Wash the mushrooms, cut into leaves and sprinkle with lemon juice. Cook the breast fillets in hot butter for 5 minutes on each side, until golden brown, and keep warm on a plate. Add butter to the pan, add the finely-diced onions and saute until glazed. Add the mushrooms, caper and wine and stew everything for 8 minutes. Combine the cream or condensed milk and the cornstarch; blend into the sauce and let it boil up once. Add the grated Gouda cheese and, if desired, salt and chopped parsley.

SPANISH CHICKEN CASSEROLE

4 chicken legs,	2 fresh green peppers
salt, pepper	4 peeled tomatoes
paprika, thyme	1 can petite peas (14 oz.)
3 tbsps. vegetable oil	1 cup cubed Gouda cheese
3 medium onions	
1 cup long-grain rice	
3 cups broth	

Thaw chicken legs in the refrigerator overnight. Rub the seasonings into the skin and cook in hot vegetable oil on all sides until golden brown. Cut the onion into rings and add to the pan. Saute until golden-yellow, and add the rice. Fill the pan with boiling broth. Let the rice simmer on low heat for 15 minutes. Wash the peppers and cut into strips, cut the peeled tomatoes into eighths and add to the rice. After 8 minutes, add the drained peas and cubed cheese. Combine carefully, season to taste and serve.

CITRUS CHICKEN

2–3 pound chicken	4 tbsps. butter
juice from 2 large lemons	1 cup long-grain rice
salt	2 cups broth
dash of parsley	⅓ cup grated coconut
2 tbsps. vegetable oil	2 bananas
	½ cup grated Gouda cheese

Remove the chicken from the package and thaw in the refrigerator overnight in a covered bowl. Divide into large pieces, rub in the lemon juice and set it back in the refrigerator for 30 minutes to allow the lemon juice to soak through. Blot the chicken dry, rub in the salt and parsley, and cook in heated vegetable oil on all sides until golden brown. Add the butter, shake in the dry rice, let it brown for 3–4 minutes and add the broth. Let it simmer for 20 minutes. The liquid should be absorbed and the rice fluffed up and dry. With forks, fold in the grated coconut, remaining lemon juice and sliced bananas. top with the grated Gouda cheese and let it cook for 5 minutes, covered to allow the cheese to melt.

CHICKEN IN AN EARTHEN POT

1 3-lb. chicken	3 onions
salt	1 bunch parsley
pepper	2 lbs. of canned corn
paprika	1 cup Gouda cheese
oregano	
9 oz. mixed dried fruit	

Remove the chicken from the package and let it thaw overnight in the refrigerator, covered. Then rub in the seasonings. Set an earthen pot in cold water for 20 minutes. Cut the onions into fourths, wash the parsley and stuff into the chicken. Close the opening with 2–3 pins. Drain the corn well, and cut the cheese into narrow strips. Layer the dried fruit, corn and cheese in the pot, and season with a dash of salt. Set the chicken on top, cover, and set into a cold oven. Set the oven to 400 degrees. Bake for 2 hours; uncover the last 10–15 minutes so that the meat will turn perfectly brown and crispy.

RICE PLATTER "SURINAM"

Cheese Rice:	Stuffed Peaches:
1½ cup long-grain rice	4 peach halves
1½ tsp. salt	6 oz. celery slices
2–3 drops saffron	1 small pkg. frozen shrimp
3 tbsps. butter	
1 tsp. curry powder	Warm Sauce:
⅔ cup Gouda cheese	6 tbsps. mayonnaise
	1 tsp. ketchup
Chicken Fillets:	a few sprays dill
4 chicken breasts	
butter	
1 orange slice for garnishing	
1 cocktail cherry for garnishing	

In 12 cups boiling salted water, add the saffron and rice, and boil uncovered for 15 minutes. Shake onto a sieve and drain well. In the same pan, heat the butter and add the curry. Pour in the rice, stir well, and let dry in a pre-heated oven for a few minutes. Cube the Gouda cheese.

In a frying pan, cook the partially-thawed chicken breast fillets in hot butter on both sides for 10 miutes, until golden brown. Remove the breasts and keep warm. Drain the peaches well and, along with the cubed celery and thawed shrimp, heat them in the frying pan. Stuff each peach half with celery and shrimp. Set a small mound of rice and blended cheese onto a pre-warmed platter. Lay the chicken fillets on top. Place the stuffed peach halves onto small rice mounds. Pour the warmed and seasoned mayonnaise over the chicken and peaches. Garnish with sprays of dill, orange slices and cocktail cherries. Serve immediately. Note: Warm the mayonnaise carefully, while constantly stirring.

STUFFED CHICKEN

1 roasting chicken	½ tsp. caraway
pepper	2½ oz. cubed cheese
onion	2 tbsps. sherry
1¼ tbsps. butter	¾ cup water
3 oz. mushrooms	½ cup double cream
10 olives	salt to taste
3 large sweet gherkins	
1 tbsp. capers	
¼ cup raisins	
½ tsp. nutmeg	
½ teaspoon thyme	

Rub the chicken with pepper and saute the chopped onion in the butter. Stir in the washed, sliced mushrooms, sliced olives, sliced pickled gherkins, capers, raisins and seasonings. Simmer for 10 minutes and then stir in the cheese and the sherry. Stuff the chicken with this mixture and keep any leftovers for the sauce. Skewer the chicken to prevent the stuffing from coming out and grill on a spit for about one hour. Add the water to the remaining stuffing, heat through, stirring continuously. Finally, stir in the cream and season to taste.

CHICKEN LIVERS IN CAPER SAUCE

¾ lb. chicken livers	1 onion
flour	1 tbsp. butter
celery salt	1 tbsp. mustard
pepper	thyme
salt	4 oz. sour cream
ground paprika	1 tbsp. capers

Halve the chicken livers, coat with flour and seasonings. Chop the onion and saute in the butter. Add the chicken livers, mustard, thyme and a little water and cook for 5 minutes. Stir some of the hot sauce into the sour cream, then pour it back into the pan. Stir in the capers, and simmer until the livers are cooked through.

CHICKEN IN THE PAN

4 chicken legs	2 green peppers
salt	2 tomatoes
2 tsps. ground paprika	½ tbsp. flour
1½ oz. butter	4 oz. sour cream
2 large onions	pepper
1 cup warm water	

Sprinkle the chicken legs with salt and ground paprika. Fry them golden brown on all sides in the melted and slightly browned butter (about 10 minutes). Fry the chopped onion in the same pan for another 10 minutes. Remove the seeds and white pith from the peppers and cut into small pieces. Peel the tomatoes and chop, also into small pieces. Add the chopped pepper and tomato to the chicken and braise for a further 15 minutes. Blend the flour with the sour cream, add a little of the hot pan juices, then pour it back into the pan, stirring continuously. Simmer for a few minutes longer, then season to taste with salt and pepper. Serve the chicken in the pan.

STEWS AND CASSEROLES

There are so many advantages to stews and casseroles as a main dish that it is hard to list them all. Perhaps the two best reasons are that stews and casseroles make inexpensive main dishes and that the leftovers, particularly when heated in the microwave, taste just as delicious (and sometimes more delicious) on the second day.

Tips for Stews and Casseroles

—For thickening ingredients in casseroles, use egg milk and sauce; for loosening the mixture, use beaten egg whites.

—Be sure to do all seasoning before baking a casserole; after baking is completed no taste can be added or removed.

—It is wise nowadays to cook with dishes that are compatible with both oven and microwave. Originals and leftovers can thus be kept in the same dish; clean-up also becomes much easier this way.

—To prevent casseroles from sticking to the dish, butter the dish and sprinkle flour over the bottom.

—For moistness, cover the surface of the casserole with daubs of butter; these will melt through the mixture during baking.

—Always set a casserole on the lower oven rack. Baking time for most casseroles is 30 minutes at 350 to 425 degrees in a pre-heated oven.

SHORT CUT HUNTER'S STEW

4 onions	8 large potatoes
2 cloves garlic	1 cup milk
1 tbsp. butter	1 egg
9 oz. lean minced meat	pepper
salt	nutmeg
pepper	3 oz. aged cheese
worcestershire sauce	2 large apples
thyme	
marjoram	

Chop the onions and saute in butter until transparent, together with the crushed garlic. Stir in the minced meat and mix with a fork until the meat is lightly cooked—add the salt and seasonings to taste. Heat the boiled potatoes in the milk and whip into a light puree with the egg, pepper, nutmeg and grated cheese (reserve a little for the garnish). Put a layer of puree into a buttered oven-proof dish, arrange half the sliced apple on top, then the minced meat, another layer of apples and finally the rest of the potato puree. Sprinkle with the cheese reserve for this purpose and bake in the center of a pre-heated oven (400 degrees) for 20 minutes.

STEW WITH CHEESE

4 tbsps. butter	2 cups water
1 medium onion	1 cup milk
1 lb. ground beef	dash of nutmeg
salt, pepper	9 oz. beets
paprika	2 large cucumbers
½ cup broth	3 Bismark herring
instant mashed potatoes	1 cup aged Gouda cheese
(4 servings)	

Heat the butter and saute the diced onions until glazed. Add the ground beef and slowly begin to braise. Use seasonings to create a mild taste, and add ½ cup broth. Continue to braise for 8 minutes. Prepare mashed potatoes as directed. Cube the red beets, cucumbers, herring and cheese and blend, along with the ground beef, into the mashed potatoes.

FRISIAN HUNTING DISH

3½ tbsps. butter	2 cups water
1 cup onions	1 cup milk
1 cup savoy cabbage	1 tbsp. butter
5 tbsps. broth or water	salt, nutmeg
instant mashed potatoes	1 cup pimento cheese
(4 servings)	

Cut onions in half, wash the cabbage and cut into strips, and begin to stew both in hot butter. Add a little water and stew until it is almost done, about 15 minutes. Prepare mashed potatoes according to directions. Put half of the mashed potatoes, along with the lightly-seasoned savoy cabbage/onion mixture, into a buttered, heat-resistant pan. Grate the cheese and sprinkle ¾ of it over the layered mass. Then spread the remaining mashed potatoes over it and sprinkle with the rest of the cheese. Bake the hunting dish in a preheated oven at 350 degrees for 20 minutes.

SPICY APRICOT STEW

1¼ lb. beef	4 medium onions
6 cups water	1 lb. potatoes
1 onion	½ lb. tomatoes
clove, bay leaf, pimento	black pepper to taste
salt	1 cup aged Gouda cheese
⅓ cup dried apricots	1 tsp. butter
3½ tbsps. butter	

Add the beef and spices (onion, clove, bay leaf, pimento, salt) into boiling water, and simmer over low heat for ½ hour. Set the apricots in 1 cup of lukewarm water and let it simmer for 1 hour. Saute 2 finely diced onions in hot butter until glazed. Add 4 cups of the beef broth to the onions. Peel the potatoes, cut into small cubes and boil for 10 minutes in the broth. Then add the apricots along with the remaining soaking water and skinned and halved tomatoes. Cook the stew for 15 minutes, or until done. Remove the meat, cut into cubes and put back into the pan. Season with pepper and serve the stew in soup cups. Cut the remaining 2 onions in half, saute in butter until glazed. Add them to stew and sprinkle heavily with grated Gouda cheese. Bake in a pre-heated oven at 400 degrees for 5 minutes until cheese begins to melt.

COUSCOUS "AFRICAN QUEEN"

1 lb. couscous (grits)	1¼ lb. chicken
2 cups water	1 carrot
salt	3 large onions
3 oz. butter	2 cups broth
5 tbsps. veg. oil	¾ cup young Gouda
½ clove garlic	salt
1 fresh green pepper	cayenne pepper
1 pepperoni	1 tsp. paprika powder
2 tomatoes	
1⅔ cans chick-peas	

Put the grits into a wide pan. Moisten with 1 cup lukewarm lightly-salted water and let it simmer for 5 minutes. Pour into a sieve and hang the sieve over a pot with boiling water. The moisture should pass through the grits. After 20 minutes, put the grits into a pan, grind down with your hands and moisten with the other cup of water. Once again, set onto the sieve and let it cook from the steam below for 15 minutes. Keep warm in the oven. Heat the vegetable oil in a casserole and cook the meat cut into large pieces. Braise the cleaned, cubed carrots, as well as the onions, briefly with the meat. Quench with a portion of the broth and braise until almost done. Wash the peppers and pepperoni, remove the ribs of the peppers, core the tomatoes, cut all the vegetables into large cubes and add them to the meat together with the chick-peas and cubed Gouda. Briefly cook thoroughly, season to taste and dish up into a bowl. Top with a slab of butter and serve.

FRESH SAVOY CABBAGE-CARROT STEW

3½ tbsps. butter	⅔ cup baby Gouda cheese
1 lb. pork shoulder	½ medium cabbage
salt, pepper	1 tsp. caraway seed
¼ bay leaf	3 cups broth
3 large onions	4 large potatoes
5 large carrots	

Cut the pork into 1 inch cubes and briefly fry in hot butter; subsequently add seasonings. Cut the onion into rings and slice the washed carrots. Layer on top of the meat. Slice the Gouda into strips and lay over the carrots. Finally, add the clean cabbage cut into strips and season with a dash of salt, pepper and caraway seed. Pour the broth over the mixture and cook covered over medium heat, about 40 minutes. Then grate the raw potatoes into the pan, cook for 5 minutes and serve. This stew tastes wonderful re-heated. You might want to double the recipe and freeze half.

VARIEGATED STEW

⅔ lb. beef	1 bunch parsley
1 quart water	1 bunch chives
1¼ lbs. potatoes	⅔ cup young Gouda cheese
1 small head of cauliflower	salt
1 red pepper	pepper
1 green pepper	paprika powder

Put the meat on to boil in cold water, and let it boil for 1 hour. Peel the potatoes, cut into cubes, add to the broth and boil for 10 minutes. Wash the cauliflower and separate the rosettes. Set them in cold salt water. Quarter the peppers, remove the ribs, and cut into strips. After the potatoes have been boiling for 10 minutes, add the peppers and cauliflower. Let it boil 15 minutes more. Blend in the chopped herbs and cubed cheese and season to taste.

FISHERMAN'S STEW

2 tbsps. butter	12 oz. canned corn
2 tbsps. flour	9 oz. smoked shellfish
1 cup milk	instant mashed potatoes
¼ cup grated aged Gouda	(3 servings)
1 egg yolk	3 tomatoes, peeled
salt	⅔ cup grated aged Gouda
cayenne pepper	

In a sauce pan, heat the butter, flour and milk until lightly simmering. Blend in the grated cheese, and thicken with the egg yolk. Season the sauce to taste. Grease a heat-resistant pan, pour in the drained corn. Skin and bone the fish. Pluck off medium pieces, and lay over the corn. Pour the sauce over the fish pieces, spread the mashed potatoes evenly over the sauce, and arrange the tomato wedges over the mixture, with the cuts facing downward. Sprinkle the stew heavily with Gouda cheese. Bake in pre-heated oven at 350 degrees for 25 minutes.

AMERICAN CHICKEN LIVER STEW

½ lb. chicken livers	chili powder
1 green pepper	ground paprika
1 red pepper	worcestershire sauce
1 onion	seasoned salt
1 clove garlic	8 oz. canned corn
2 tbsps. butter	8 oz. canned peas
1 small can tomato puree	3 oz. aged cheese
salt and pepper	parsley
tabasco sauce	

Clean the livers. Wash the peppers, remove the seeds and pith and chop finely. Chop up the onion and garlic. Fry the chicken livers in butter until brown, then add the onion, garlic and peppers. Saute for 5 minutes, then stir in the tomato puree, salt and seasonings. Drain the corn and peas, add to the livers with a little of the corn liquid if necessary. Stir in the peeled, sliced tomatoes, the grated cheese and the chopped parsley, in that order. Heat thoroughly and serve at once.

"HEAVEN AND EARTH"
(With A Sausage Wreath)

2 lbs. potatoes	pinch of sugar
2 lbs. bitter apples	4 tbsps. butter
½ tsp. salt	½ cup grated cheese

Wash and peel the potatoes. Cube, and add to a pan ½ full of water. Boil for 5–6 minutes. Add the peeled, cubed apples, season and boil 10 minutes longer. Whip everything together until a mash develops, but it should not be fully smooth. If necessary, add a little more water or broth. Blend in the butter and grated Gouda cheese. Excellent with the sausage wreath below.

SAUSAGE WREATH

1 sausage ring	¼ cup smoked, lean bacon
1 large onion	butter for spreading
1 large apple	paprika for sprinkling
½ cup aged Gouda cheese	

Remove the skin from the sausage and cut slits into it. Cut the onions into thicker half-moons, pare the apple into eighths and bacon into 1 in. squares. Stuff the ingredients alternately into the slits in the sausage, daub everything with melted butter and broil for 10–15 minutes under the pre-heated broiler. Sprinkle with paprika. Serve with "Heaven and Earth" in the center of the wreath.

SEMOLINA DUMPLING IN HERB SAUCE

3 cups water	Sauce:
3 tbsps. butter	3 tsps. butter
pinch of salt	3 tbsps. flour
9 oz. semolina	1 cup broth
3 eggs	1 cup milk
½ cup grated aged Gouda	1 egg yolk
peppermill	pinch of salt
pinch of nutmeg	1 tsp. lemon juice
¼ cup cubed Edam cheese	dash of pepper
¼ cup smoked, lean bacon	1 bunch chives
	1 bunch parsley
	few sprigs dill

Bring water, butter and salt to a boil. Strew in the semolina, and cook. Let it cook down somewhat, gradually fold in the eggs and grated Gouda cheese. Add spices, and season to taste. Shape into dumplings with moist hands. Press the bacon and Edam cheese cubes into each dumpling. Cook thoroughly in boiling saltwater, and drain. Prepare the herb sauce and pour over the dumplings.

PARIS CHEESE DUMPLINGS

Dough:	Sauce:
1¼ cups water	3 tbsp. butter
pinch of salt	3 medium onions
½ cup butter	½ cup ketchup
½ cup flour	½ cup cream
5 eggs	peppermill
½ cup grated aged Gouda	pinch of salt
7–8 cups saltwater for boiling	½ cup grated aged Gouda

Bring water and salt to a boil, and remove from heat. Add all the flour and butter at once. Set the pot onto the burner again and make a dumpling. Let cool. Blend in the eggs one after the other, and add the grated cheese. With 2 teaspoons, put the dough into simmering saltwater. Simmer the dumplings for 10 minutes. In the meantime, saute the diced onions in butter until light yellow. Add ketchup, cream, seasonings. Season the sauce to taste. Grease large heat-resistant cookie sheet, and with a skimmer, remove the dumplings from the saltwater and set onto the baking sheet. Pour the sauce over the dumplings and top heavily with grated mature Gouda cheese. Bake in a pre-heated oven at 400 degrees for 15–20 minutes.

CORN CASSEROLE

1 cup cream	1 tsp. soy sauce
2 eggs, divided	1 can crabmeat (7 oz.)
dash of salt, pepper	⅔ cup cubed Gouda
1 can mushrooms	1 fresh green pepper
1 can corn	

In a bowl, whisk cream, egg yolks and seasonings until well-blended. Drain the corn and mushrooms, as well as the crabmeat and add them to the mixture, along with the cubed cheese. Wash the green pepper and cut into narrow strips, and blend into the mixture. Beat the egg whites until stiff and fold into the mixture. Pour into a greased, heat-resistant pan and bake for 40 minutes at 375 degrees.

COUNTRY BEAN CASSEROLE

3 tbsps. butter	2 tbsps. ketchup
1 onion	salt
1½ cup ground beef and pork	1 tsp. paprika
4 tomatoes, peeled	instant mashed potatoes
1 can cut green beans	(4 servings)
	⅔ cup aged grated Gouda

Heat the butter, saute the diced onion until glazed. Add the ground beef and pork and braise. Slice the peeled tomatoes into eighths and drain the beans. Add to the meat. Season to taste. Prepare the mashed potatoes as directed. Grease a heat-resistant pan, add a layer of mashed potatoes, and pour over the meat-vegetable mixture. Top with more mashed potatoes and sprinkle with grated mature Gouda cheese. Brown in a pre-heated oven at 400 degrees for 15–20 minutes.

SAUERKRAUT ROYALE

2 lbs. potatoes	Cheese Sauce:
salt	1 oz. butter
1 tbsp. butter	1 oz. flour
milk	1¼ cups milk
pepper	3 oz. aged cheese
nutmeg	pepper
1 lb. sauerkraut	ground paprika
8 slices ham	

Peel and boil the potatoes in salted water until tender. Mash with the butter and milk until light and smooth. Season with salt, pepper and nutmeg and spoon into a buttered oven-proof dish. Cook the sauerkraut for 10 minutes, drain well and roll up in the slices of ham. Arrange them on top of the potato puree. To make the cheese sauce, melt the butter in a saucepan. Stir in the flour and then gradually add the milk, stirring continuously, until the sauce is thick and smooth. Stir in three-quarters of the grated cheese and the seasoning. Pour the cheese sauce over the ham rolls and cover with the rest of the grated cheese. Place the dish in a pre-heated oven (400 degrees) for about 20 minutes until the top is golden brown.

CHEESE AND VEGETABLE RATATOUILLE

½ head of cabbage	3 oz. ham
2 onions	3 oz. grated aged cheese
2 tbsps. butter	1 tbsp. chopped parsley
1½ lbs. potatoes	salt
½ cup water	pepper
salt	garlic powder
½ cucumber	thyme
2 tomatoes	seasoned salt

Wash and slice the cabbage and saute with the finely chopped onion in butter for 5 minutes. Add the cubed potatoes, water and salt and cook the potatoes for 15 minutes. Add the cucumber slices for the last 5 minutes of the cooking time. Remove from the heat, stir in the sliced tomatoes, the chopped ham and cheese, and finely-chopped parsley. Season to taste with the salt, pepper and other seasonings.

CHEESY SHEPHERD'S PIE

1½ oz. bacon	2 large onions
8 oz. lean meat	5 oz. mushrooms
salt, pepper	3 oz. grated cheese
nutmeg	1½ lbs. potatoes
celery salt	milk
2 tbsps. butter	nutmeg
	butter

Cut the bacon into squares and fry slowly until crisp. Crumble the meat in the pan, stir until it is light brown and add the salt and other seasonings. Melt the butter in a pan, saute the chopped onions in it, add the washed and sliced mushrooms and saute for a further 5 minutes. Fill a buttered oven-proof dish with layers of bacon and meat, onion and mushrooms and cheese. Reserve a little cheese for the top. Top with a layer of creamy mashed potatoes. Sprinkle with the cheese, put aside for this purpose, and place the dish in the upper part of a pre-heated oven (400 degrees) for about 20 minutes until the crust is golden brown.

POTATOES, RICE AND PASTA

Until recent years, these groups of complex starches and carbohydrates were given short shrift. We believed that they were the fattening foods; that a potato was a definite no on a diet, that pasta was the ruination of the female figure and that rice was a flavorless food to be largely ignored.

Now, however, we know just how wrong we were. These dishes contain the complex carbohydrates and low calories necessary to maintain a high energy level while still eating light and healthy meals. In addition, they are rich in fiber, which aids digestion, and can be fixed in so many ways that they add infinite variety to the diet.

POTATOES

—There are more than 100 varieties of potato on the market and the average potato has only 100 calories.

—Potato maturity has three gradations; new, semi-early and late. New potatoes are simply washed and brushed with butter before baking. They are delicious, but do not keep long. Semi-early potatoes and late potatoes will keep longer.

—Store potatoes in a cool, dark, dry spot and make sure that they are well-ventilated. Do not store potatoes in the refrigerator.

—Peel potatoes just prior to boiling and do not let them sit long in the water.

—Try dressing simple baked potatoes with condiments other than sour cream or butter. Mustard makes a delicious dressing as does low-fat yogurt mixed with herbs. Experiment with your own combinations to keep the calories low and the taste unique.

HOPPELPOPPEL
(Fried Potatoes With Ham And Eggs)

2 lbs. firm potatoes	⅔ cup middle-aged Gouda
4 tbsps. butter	4 eggs
2 medium onions	½ cup milk
⅔ cup cooked ham	½ bunch parsley
4 oz. can mushrooms	1 bunch chives
salt	¼ cup aged Gouda
pepper	

Boil the potatoes, unpeeled, for 25–30 minutes. Drain the water, remove the potatoes and let cool. Grease a heat-resistant pan. Heat the butter in a frying pan, saute the diced onions and cubed ham. Add the drained mushrooms, and stew for 5–8 minutes. Add the spices and season to taste. Slice the potatoes, unpeeled, and arrange one layer into the pan, along with coarsely-grated middle-aged Gouda cheese. Whisk the eggs, milk and chopped herbs. Pour over the potatoes. Sprinkle with grated mature Gouda cheese and brown in a pre-heated oven at 425 degrees for 30 minutes. Serve hot.

POTATO CAKES WITH CORNED BEEF

1 onion	8 slices corned beef
1 bunch chives	4 slices baby Gouda cheese
2 cups water	ketchup
1 pkg. potato pancake batter	

Chop the onions, dice the chives finely, and add to the water for making the mashed potatoes. Stir this mixture and let it boil up. Heat the vegetable oil in a frying pan, cook small potato pancakes and keep warm. Cover ½ of each pancake with a slice of corned beef and cheese. Top with a dollop of ketchup and fold over the other half of the cake.

POTATO PANCAKES EDAM

1 pkg. potato pancake batter (for 15 pancakes)
⅔ cup Edam cheese
vegetable oil for frying

Make the contents of the package as directed. Cut the Edam cheese into mini cubes or grate coarsely. Let the mixture swell up over heat. In a frying pan, add oil and let it heat up vigorously. Spoon in the batter, stroke until smooth, and fry on both sides until crispy-brown. Serve hot with sugar, apple sauce, preserves or mild mustard.

BROWNED POTATOES

2 lbs. potatoes	peppermill
4 tbsps. butter	4 peeled tomatoes
2 medium onions	1 cup middle-aged Gouda
½ tsp. salt	a bunch chives
dash of oregano	

Wash and peel the potatoes, cut into thin slices, and blot dry. Melt the butter in a frying pan and add the potatoes. Cut the onions into rings or half-moons, arrange over the potatoes. Lightly salt. Cook the potatoes until light-yellow in color. Cover, and let it simmer for 5 more minutes. Flip over with a spatula and let the other side also turn golden yellow and crispy. Season with oregano and pepper. Cut the tomatoes into eighths and the cheese into small squares and lay over the potatoes. Cook for 3–4 minutes, blend carefully and serve with diced chives.

POTATO SOUFFLE

2 lbs. mashing potatoes	½ tsp. salt
5 tbsps. butter	pepper
4 eggs, divided	dash of nutmeg
1 cup cream	
½ cup grated middle-aged Gouda	

Boil the potatoes, unpeeled, until done. Peel, mash, and blend with butter, egg yolks, cream, coarsely-grated Gouda cheese and seasonings until foamy. Beat the egg whites until stiff and blend into the mixture. Grease a heat-resistant pan, pour in the foamy potato mixture and bake in a pre-heated oven at 350 degrees for 30–40 minutes.

BAKED POTATO ROSETTES

2 lbs. mashing potatoes	3 eggs
dash of salt	dash of nutmeg
⅔ cup butter	

Wash the potatoes and peel. Boil in saltwater until done. Drain the water, let the steam out and mash the potatoes. Blend in the butter, gradually add the eggs and season with nutmeg. The mixture has to be smooth and glossy. Preheat the oven to 400 degrees. Lightly grease the baking sheet. Spoon the potato mixture onto the sheet or squirt out small rosettes with a decorating gun. Bake until golden yellow for 10–15 minutes and serve immediately. Serves 6.

BROWNED MUSHROOMS IN POTATO WREATH

1½ lbs. fresh mushrooms	instant mashed potatoes
3 tbsps. butter	(4 servings)
pinch of salt	2 tbsps. butter
pinch of white pepper	2 eggs
2—3 tbsps. lemon juice	½ cup mature grated Gouda

Wash the mushrooms thoroughly, and cut into leaves. Heat the butter, add the mushrooms with seasonings and lemon juice, and stew for 5—8 minutes. Prepare the mashed potatoes as directed, and blend in the butter and whole eggs. In a greased, heat-resistant pan, form a wreath from the mashed potatoes or squirt the potatoes from a decorating gun into the shape of a wreath. Put the mushrooms in the center and sprinkle with grated Gouda cheese. Let it bake until golden-yellow in a pre-heated oven at 400 degrees for 10—15 minutes.

DUTCH "STIMPSTAMP"
(National Potato Dish In Holland)

1½ pounds chicory	3 tbsps. butter
4 lbs. mashing potatoes	pinch of nutmeg
½ tsp. salt	1 cup baby Gouda cheese
1 cup milk	

Wash the chicory thoroughly, cut into ½-inch wide strips and drain well on a sieve. Wash and peel the potatoes, cut into uniform pieces and boil thoroughly in a little saltwater. Pour out the water, let it steam out well and mash. Add hot milk, butter, nutmeg, and whisk until foamy. Immediately before serving, blend the chicory into the mashed potatoes and season to taste.

POTATO CROQUETTES

1 lb. potatoes	1½ oz. aged cheese
1½ oz. butter	1 tbsp. flour
2 eggs	parsley
salt	breadcrumbs
nutmeg	
grated rind of 1 lemon	

Cook the potatoes in a little boiling salted water, drain and rub through a sieve. Stir in the butter, beaten egg yolks, salt, nutmeg, grated lemon rinds, grated cheese, flour and chopped parsley. Shape into croquettes using 2 spoons, dip into the lightly beaten egg white, and roll in bread crumbs (repeat this procedure twice). Deep fry the croquettes until golden brown.

FRIED PARSLEY POTATO BALLS

1 lb. small new potatoes	
2 oz. butter	
1 bunch parsley	

Boil the washed and scraped potatoes in a little salted water for 5 minutes. Add finely chopped parsley and mix well. Drain and fry in the butter until golden brown and cooked through. The potatoes can also be used raw in which case they will need approximately 15 minutes frying time so that they are cooked through and golden brown.

CUMIN POTATOES

2 lbs. potatoes	cumin powder
2 tbsps. butter	¾ pound young cheese
salt	

Scrub the potatoes well but do not peel them. Dry and cut through the middle. Brush the cut side with a little melted butter, sprinkle with salt and cumin seeds. Put the potato halves onto a buttered baking sheet, and put them into the middle of a pre-heated oven (475 degrees) and roast for about 30 minutes until almost cooked. Make a cut in the top of each potato with a knife, insert a small piece of cheese and return the potatoes to the oven until the cheese begins to melt.

CHEESY POTATOES

2 lbs. potatoes
6 oz. mature cheese
2 tbsps. butter

Scrub the potatoes, boil them in the skins until tender, peel and cut into thick slices. Layer them up, alternately, with layers of grated cheese, in a buttered ovenproof dish. Dot with butter, place in the upper part of a pre-heated oven (450 degrees) for 10–15 minutes and bake until top is light golden brown.

WESTPHALIAN POTATO CAKES

2 lbs. potatoes	flour
2–3 eggs	lard for frying
½ lb. aged cheese	chopped parsley
salt	
black pepper	

Boil the potatoes until tender, drain carefully and mash well (the potatoes must be as dry as possible). Beat the eggs and stir them together with the grated cheese, into the potatoes. Season to taste with salt and pepper. Knead the mixture well to make a stiff dough, adding a little flour if necessary. With a tablespoon, shape into flat round cakes, dip into flour and deep fry until golden brown. Drain the potato cakes on absorbent paper and sprinkle with chopped parsley. Alternately, the parsley can be stirred in to the dough before frying.

RICE

—In recent years, rice has become a favored mealtime addition. The market is filled with rice dishes ranging from plain instant white rice and unpolished brown rice to rice in sauces, mixed with vegetables and seasoned with herbs and spices.

—Rice is wonderful for the digestive system, providing natural starches and fiber. In fact, in countries where fish and rice are the dietary staples, there is a correspondingly low incidence of heart disease and cancer.

—Slow-cooking rices are cooked in the following manner:

Water Rice. Bring 8–10 cups water with 1 tsp. salt to a boil. Add 1 heaping cup of rice. Let it boil uncovered for 12–15 minutes. Drain the water, steam out the rice, and let dry well.

Swelling Rice. (rice that doubles or triples in size when cooked). Bring 4 cups water with 1 tsp. salt to a boil, and add 2 cups rice. Cover, and cook on low heat for 20 minutes; all liquid should be absorbed.

Risotto. Heat 2 tbsps. butter, and saute 1 diced onion until glazed. Saute 2 cups rice with the onion and pour in 4 cups broth. Cover, and cook on low heat for 20 minutes.

Creamed Rice. Bring to a boil 4 cups milk with 2 tbsps. butter, 1 small piece lemon peel, 1 vanilla bean, 1 pinch of salt. Add 7 oz. round-grain rice and 1 tbsp. sugar, and cook on low heat or in the oven for 35 minutes. Remove the lemon peel and vanilla bean. Serve with sugar and cinnamon.

VEGETABLE-RISOTTO

1 lb. fresh green peppers	3 cups broth, dash of salt
2 medium onions	1 tsp. paprika
3 tbsps. butter	dash of white pepper
1 cup long-grain rice	⅔ cup cubed Gouda

Wash the peppers and cut into strips. In butter, saute together with the onions, cut into half-moons. Add the rice. Stew while constantly stirring for 5–8 minutes and pour in the boiling broth. Add seasonings and simmer on low heat for 15 minutes. Blend in the cubed cheese. Season to taste and serve.

PAELLA ESPANOL

1 cup frozen peas	1 cup long-grain rice
1 cup frozen green beans	dash of saffron
1 clove garlic	2 cups broth
5 tbsps. vegetable oil	8 oz. fish (codfish)
1 small chicken	3 peeled tomatoes
1 large onion	7 oz. crab or shrimp
1 green pepper	1 can clams (7 oz.)
1 red pepper	1 cup cubed Gouda cheese

Boil the frozen vegetables in 1 cup lightly salted water for 10–15 minutes. Drain well. Rub a large, heavy frying pan with the garlic clove, heat the vegetable oil, and cook the chicken carved into small pieces, the skin removed, until golden brown. Chop the onion coarsely, the peppers into strips, and add them together with the rice into the pan with the chicken. Stew for 8 minutes. Sprinkle with saffron and pour in the broth. Simmer for 10 minutes more, until thoroughly cooked. Top with the large fish pieces; add the tomatoes cut into eighths and stew for 10 more minutes. Finally, blend in the cubed Gouda cheese, season to taste, set the pan on the table and serve.

RICE WITH LIVER-APPLE FILLING

10 oz. Italian Avorio rice	2 cups milk
2 tbsps. butter	2 eggs
½ cup smoked, lean bacon	salt
1 large onion	nutmeg
7 oz. beef liver	2—3 tbsps. breadcrumbs
2 medium apples	2 tbsps. butter for daubing
¼ tsp. marjoram	
dash of salt	
⅔ cup of Edam cheese	

Pour the rice into boiling saltwater and let it boil up, uncovered, for 12–15 minutes. Steam out and drain well. Melt the butter, and saute the cubed bacon and chopped onion. Cut the liver into strips, and the apples into small slices, and fry with the bacon and onion. Season to taste. Grate the Edam cheese, and prepare an egg-milk mixture from milk, eggs and spices. Grease a heat-resistant pan, and alternately layer the rice, grated cheese and liver mixture in single layers. Top with the rice, pour over the egg-milk mixture, sprinkle with breadcrumbs and daub with butter. Pre-heat the oven to 400 degrees and bake for 20 minutes.

SKILLET SURPRISE

3 tbsps. butter	2 pimentos
5 oz. bacon	dash of salt
4 large onions	pepper
7 oz. baby Gouda cheese	4 slices codfish
2 cups broth	(5 oz. each)
½ bay leaf	juice from ½ lemon

Set the skillet in cold water for 30 minutes. Heat the butter and saute the cubed bacon briefly. Dice the onions, cut the leaf into half-moons, and grate the carrots and celery. Stew these ingredients with the bacon. Layer the raw rice, cubed Gouda cheese, and vegetables lengthwise into the skillet. Pour over the broth with the seasonings. Sprinkle the fish with drops of lemon juice and lay over the mixture. Cover and cook thoroughly in the oven set at 425 degrees for 45–50 minutes.

RANGOON RICE

1 small chicken	10 maraschino cherries
⅓ cup butter	½ cup unsalted cashew nuts
2 tsps. curry	⅔ cup middle-aged Gouda
3 medium onions	½ tsp. paprika powder
1 cup Patna or Avorio rice	pinch of cayenne pepper
3 cups broth	dash of salt
5 tbsps. mandarin wedges	2 tbsps. chili sauce
5 tbsps. small pineapple chunks	

Thaw the chicken. Cut in half, remove the skin, and pluck off as much meat from the bones as possible. Heat the butter and add the curry. Saute the chicken pieces until golden brown on all sides. Add the diced onion and rice, and saute the chicken. Pour in the boiling broth and simmer on low heat for 10 minutes. Then add the drained mandarins, pineapple chunks and halved cherries, as well as the cashew kernels cut in half lengthwise. Also add the cubed Gouda cheese. Season to taste with the spices.

BELGIAN RICE-CHEESE CAKE

Ingredients:	Angel Food Crust:
1 tbsp. butter	7 oz. flour
1 tbsp. flour	1 egg
½ cup milk	pinch of salt
pinch of salt	½ cup butter
white pepper	
dash nutmeg	
1 egg yolk	
5 tbsps. boiled long-grain rice	
4 tbsps. frozen peas	
4 tbsps. frozen carrots	
½ cup middle-aged Gouda	
1 egg white	

Sift flour into a bowl. Set daubs of egg, salt and butter on top. Knead the dough and refrigerate for 15 minutes. Spread ⅔ of the dough over the bottom of an ungreased round cake pan (9 inches) and lightly tap the dough with the fork a few times. Shape the remaining dough into a roll, lay around the edges of the pan and press into place with a fork. Pre-bake the crust in a pre-heated oven at 350 degrees for 15 minutes.

Lightly simmer the butter and flour. Pour in the milk, season with salt and nutmeg and thicken with the egg yolk. Blend in the boiled rice, the 5-minute stewed frozen vegetables and the cubed Gouda cheese. Beat the egg white until stiff and fold into the mixture. Pour the ingredients onto the bottom crust and bake thoroughly at 400 degrees for 30 minutes.

FLORENTINE RISOTTO

¼ cup butter	white pepper
1 medium onion	3 peeled tomatoes
1 cup Italian Avorio rice	4 oz. cooked ham
3 cups broth, salt	1 cup middle-aged Gouda
15 oz. frozen spinach	3 eggs
dash of nutmeg	5 tbsps. condensed milk

Heat butter in a heat-resistant pan with a cover. Saute the finely-diced onion until light yellow. Add rice and saute with the onions while constantly stirring. Pour in the hot broth, season with salt, cover, and simmer on low heat for 20 minutes. Prepare the frozen spinach as directed, and season. Slice the tomatoes into eighths, ham into strips and the Gouda cheese into cubes. Beat the eggs with milk. Combine all ingredients with the spinach. Season to taste, and pour over the rice mixture. Bake in a pre-heated oven at 400 degrees for 25 minutes.

FRIED RICE CAKES

½ cup milk	½ bunch parsley
3 tbsps. flour	6 tbsps. boiled long-grain
2 eggs	rice
salt	3 oz. sliced mushrooms
pepper	½ cup middle-aged Gouda
dash of nutmeg	vegetable oil for frying

Stir the flour into the milk. Add eggs and seasonings. Work everything to a smooth batter. Blend in the chopped parsley, boiled rice, mushrooms and cubed Gouda cheese. Let the mixture stand for 5 minutes before frying. Heat the vegetable oil and make small, round cakes, golden yellow in color on each side.

RISOTTO MILANESE

1 onion	pinch of turmeric
1 pepper	2 tomatoes
2 tbsps. butter	3 oz. mushrooms
8 oz. ground meat	seasoned salt
6 oz. rice	rosemary
1½ cups water	3 oz. aged cheese
1 bouillon cube	

Chop the onion, remove the seeds and white pith from the pepper and cut into small pieces. Saute in the butter, add the meat, stir and cook until the meat is light brown in color—separate with a fork. Add the dry unwashed rice and fry until golden brown. Dissolve the bouillon cube in the water, pour into the risotto, add the turmeric and cook for 20 minutes until the rice is tender. Add the sliced tomatoes and mushrooms for the last five minutes of the cooking time. Season the risotto with aroma salt and the rosemary and add salt if required. Remove from the heat and stir in the grated cheese.

RICE AND LEEK AU GRATIN

6½ oz. rice	Sauce:
1½ cups water	2 tbsps. butter
1 bouillon cube	2 tbsps. flour
3 leeks	1½ cups milk
2 tbsps. butter	seasoned salt
2 tsps. curry powder	salt and pepper
	6 oz. aged cheese

Cook the rice in the water flavored with a bouillon cube until the rice is dry and tender (about 20 minutes) Wash and cut the leeks into neat pieces, re-wash then braise in the butter with the curry powder for 10 minutes. For the sauce, melt the butter, stir in the flour, and gradually add the milk stirring continuously, until the sauce is smooth and thick. Season to taste. Fill a buttered oven-proof dish with layers of rice, leeks and slices of cheese in that order. The last layer should be rice. Cover with the sauce and bake for 20 minutes in a pre-heated oven (425 degrees) until the top is golden brown.

FRIED RICE

1 clove garlic	1 green pepper
2 onions	salt
1½ tbsps. butter	1¼ cups water
6 oz. rice	1 bouillon cube

Fry the finely-chopped garlic and chopped onions in the butter. Stir in the uncooked rice and fry gently. Add the finely-chopped, de-seeded pepper, salt, water and bouillon cube and cook over low heat until the rice is tender (about 20 minutes).

GOURMET RICE

1¼ cup water	6 oz. Leiden cheese
salt	8 oz. sour cream
6 oz. rice	celery salt
1 green pepper	basil
1 red pepper	onion salt
2 tbsps. butter	ground paprika
1 onion	1½ oz. aged cheese

Bring the lightly salted water to the boil. Add the rice, stir once, cover and cook on the lowest heat possible until tender and dry (approximately 20 minutes) Chop the peppers and onion and saute in the butter. Cut the cheese into small cubes and stir the cheese, the onion-pepper mixture, sour cream and seasonings into the cooked rice. Spoon the mixture into a buttered oven-proof dish, cover with grated cheese and place the dish for 20 minutes in the middle of a pre-heated oven (400 degrees) until the top is golden brown.

PASTA

—Pasta, once believed to be the premier villain in making us fat, has been thoroughly reevaluated in recent years. Pasta contains complex carbohydrates and is the food of choice for athletes, particularly close to the big race or competition.

—As a main course, 11–12 oz. should serve 4 people.

—Add the noodles to boiling saltwater; for 4 oz. you need 4 cups of water with ½ tsp. salt.

—Boil uncovered.

—Noodles should be cooked "al dente." Do not overcook them or they will be too soft.

—Add butter or a drop of oil to keep the noodles from sticking together.

MACARONI DE LUXE

¾ lb. macaroni	2 cups milk
salt	9 oz. young cheese
1 onion	pepper
1 pepper	1 tsp. worcestershire
2 tbsps. butter	4 tomatoes
2 tbsps. flour	
1 tsp. mustard powder	

Cook the macaroni in plenty of boiling salted water until tender. Drain in a colander and rinse with cold water. Chop the onion and the pepper and saute lightly in the butter. Stir in the flour and mustard powder and add the milk, stirring continuously. Boil the sauce for a few minutes. Cut half of the cheese into small pieces and stir these into the sauce. Season with salt, pepper and worcestershire sauce. Put the macaroni into a buttered oven-proof dish and cover with the cheese sauce. Cut the washed tomatoes into slices and arrange them on top. Cut the rest of the cheese into small strips and arrange them around the tomatoes. Cover the dish, and bake in the middle of a pre-heated oven (350 degrees) for 30 minutes.

HAM AND NOODLES AU GRATIN

1 large onion	pepper
2 tbsps. butter	nutmeg
2 tbsps. flour	seasoned salt
1¼ cup milk	12 oz. noodles
3 oz. mushrooms	3 oz. sliced ham
½ cup water	1½ oz. aged cheese
salt	

Saute the chopped onion in the butter. Stir in the flour and milk, continuing to stir well until the sauce is smooth and thick. Cook the washed mushrooms in the water, add the seasoning and cook for 3 minutes. Stir the mushrooms and liquid into the sauce and season to taste. Cook the noodles according to the directions on the packet. Place in a dish and cover with strips of ham. Pour the sauce over the top and sprinkle with grated cheese.

MACARONI AND FRUIT

8 oz. macaroni	salt and pepper
salt	seasoned salt
1 large pepper	thyme
2 large onions	5 oz. mushrooms
2½ tbsps. butter	1½ oz. raisins
3 oz. aged cheese	2 apples

Cook the macaroni in plenty of boiling water until tender (about 15 minutes). Then strain and rinse under the cold tap. Wash the pepper, remove the seeds and white pith and cut into small strips. Chop the onion and fry it and the pepper strips in half the butter until the onion is golden brown. Stir these vegetables and the grated cheese into the macaroni. Season to taste with salt and the other seasonings. Wash and slice the mushrooms, fry in the rest of the butter for 5 minutes until golden brown. For the last few minutes of the cooking time, add the washed raisins and the coarsely chopped apples. Spoon this mixture on top of the macaroni and sprinkle with a little extra grated cheese if wished.

GREEN RIBBON NOODLES A LA MARIETTA

½ cup mature Gouda cheese	½ cup cream
10 oz. egg-spinach noodles	1 clove garlic
3 tbsps. butter	pepper
2 medium onions	salt
½ cup ketchup	4 eggs
4–5 tbsps. broth	butter for frying

Grate the mature Gouda cheese, and serve in small bowls. Put the noodles into boiling saltwater and cook for 15 minutes. Drain, and steam out until warm. Keep warm in a pre-warmed, covered bowl. Rub the garlic clove into the pan. Melt the butter and saute the finely-diced onions until light yellow. Add ketchup, broth, cream and seasonings. Cook thoroughly, and season to taste. Cook the fried eggs in butter, then serve the noodles with grated, mature Gouda cheese and sauce.

LIP-SMACKING NOODLES

7 oz. shell noodles	3 eggs, divided
5 tbsps. butter	⅓ cup raisins
½ cup sugar	⅓ cup chopped almonds
3 tbsps. vanilla	

Cook the noodles as directed. Steam out until warm, drain and let cool. Blend the butter, sugar and vanilla until foamy. Add the egg yolks. Blend in the washed and dried raisins, chopped almonds and the noodles. Finally, beat the egg whites until stiff and fold into the mixture. Put the mixture into a greased, heat-resistant pan or into small individual pans. Bake until golden yellow at 400 degrees for 30 minutes. This dish makes a filling dessert after a small, light meal.

MACARONI GARDNER

½ cup bacon	10 oz. beef sausage
3 tbsps. butter	1 tsp. flour
2 medium onions	1 cup broth
1 leek	⅔ cup middle-aged Gouda
½ raw celery stalk	1 bunch parsley
2 carrots	10–12 oz. macaroni
dash of salt	1 tbsp. butter
white pepper	

Cube the bacon, lightly saute in hot butter. Cut the onions into half-moons and the leek in half lengthwise. Rake the celery and carrots. Braise all ingredients with the seasonings for 15 minutes. Cut the beef sausage into strips and add to the vegetables. After 5–8 minutes, add the flour, and saute. Add the broth and let it cook thoroughly. Blend in the cubed cheese and finely-chopped parsley. Meanwhile, cook the macaroni as directed. Drain, steam out until warm, run butter through the noodles and serve with the vegetable-ragout.

NOODLES WITH COTTAGE CHEESE

1 cup noodles	dash of salt
1½ lbs. cottage cheese	1 cup milk
3 eggs, divided	½ cup Edam cheese
1 tsp. paprika	2–3 tbsps. breadcrumbs
	2 tbsps. butter for daubing

Cook the noodles as directed. Drain, steam out until warm and let dry well. Beat the cottage cheese with egg yolks until creamy. Blend in the seasonings, milk and grated Edam cheese, and fold in the noodles. Beat the egg whites until stiff and blend into the noodles mixture. Grease a heat-resistant pan, pour in the cottage cheese-noodle mixture; sprinkle with breadcrumbs, daub with butter and bake in a pre-heated oven at 400 degrees for 40 minutes.

MACARONI WITH SEAFOOD

⅔ cup aged Gouda cheese	¼ tsp. oregano
3 large onions	7 oz. tuna fish
1 can peeled Italian tomatoes	7 oz. clams
dash of salt	½ cup sour cream
black pepper	1 bunch parsley
dash of rosemary	12 oz. macaroni

Grate the mature Gouda cheese, and dish into small bowls. Heat oil in a frying pan and saute the diced onions. Add tomatoes in their juice, drained and plucked tuna fish and clams. Braise vigorously. Blend in the sour cream and sprinkle with chopped parsley. Meanwhile, cook the macaroni as directed, and serve with the sauce and grated Gouda cheese.

HOMEMADE STUFFED CANNELONI

1 package canneloni (18 oz.)	3 eggs
3 tbsps. butter	salt
7 oz. ground beef	¼ tsp. oregano
2–3 oz. can concentrated	pepper
tomatoes	⅔ cup aged Gouda
7 tbsps. breadcrumbs	

Cook the canneloni in noodles in saltwater for 8–10 minutes. Steam out until warm, drain and lay out on tinfoil. For the filling, heat the butter in a pan, briefly cook the meat. Add the washed and diced spinach and cook thoroughly for 10 minutes. Add the concentrated tomatoes, and let cool. Add the breadcrumbs, eggs and seasoning. Blend well and season to taste. Spread the mixture over the canneloni, roll up, and lay on a greased, heat-resistant pan. Sprinkle heavily with grated mature Gouda cheese and brown in a pre-heated oven at 375 degrees for 15–20 minutes.

SPAGHETTI WITH MEAT SAUCE

3 tbsps. butter	½ tsp. oregano
2 large onions	1 tsp. paprika
1 cup ground beef & pork	14 oz. peeled Italian
dash of salt	tomatoes
pepper	2 tbsps. butter
	⅔ cup aged grated Gouda

Heat the butter, saute the finely-diced onions until glazed. Add ground beef, pork and spices. Braise on low heat for 10–15 minutes. Cook the spaghetti as directed, adding it to boiling saltwater and cook thoroughly. Top the meat with the tomatoes in their juice and briefly braise until done. Season to taste, and serve in a bowl. Drain the noodles, steam out with warm water. Run the noodles through melted butter and serve heavily topped with grated Gouda cheese.

SPAGHETTI MAZZOTTI

8 oz. spaghetti	1 small can tomato puree
2 bouillon cubes	seasoned salt
1½ quarts water	salt
2 onions	thyme
1 pepper	1 tbsp. butter
2 tbsps. butter	3 oz. aged cheese
8 oz. lean ground beef	

Boil the spaghetti according to the directions on the packet in a deep pan with plenty of water, flavored with the stock cubes. Peel the onions, remove the seeds and pith from the pepper, chop the onions and cut the pepper into small pieces. Melt the butter in a saucepan and heat until light brown. First, saute the onion until light brown and then add the chopped pepper. Stir in the ground beef and cook until light brown. Separate with a fork and add the tomato puree. Take out 2 ladles of stock from the spaghetti pan and add to the sauce—cook until the sauce thickens a little. Season to taste. When the spaghetti is cooked, rinse with cold water in a colander, and reheat in the same pan with butter. Put the spaghetti into a deep bowl or dish, make a hollow in the center and fill with sauce. Cover with grated cheese. Keep the dish warm as it cools rapidly.

HERB SPAGHETTI

1 small onion	3 oz. aged cheese
1 clove garlic	1 tbsp. parsley
½ tbsp. basil	6 oz. spaghetti
2 tbsps. butter	salt

Saute the chopped onion, crushed clove of garlic and finely-chopped basil in the butter. Stir this, together with the grated cheese and chopped parsley into the cooked and drained spaghetti.

VEGETABLES

Vegetables—fresh, hot or cold, steamed, stewed, or mixed in casseroles—are delicious, nutritious, easily available and inexpensive. In this section, we offer unusual vegetable dishes with that inimitable European flavor.

Vegetable Tips

—Buy fresh vegetables when they are in season.

—Water extracts vitamins and minerals from vegetables. If you intend to eat them fresh, wash quickly in cold water, then steam lightly to retain all of the nutritive qualities.

—Never over-cook vegetables. Over-cooked, they lose their flavor as well as their nutrients.

—If you are trying to avoid butter, try seasoning vegetables with herbs and a drop of wine or vinegar.

VEGETABLE DISHES

SUMMER CARROTS

1 onion	salt
2 tbsps. butter	lemon balm
1 tbsp. flour	celery salt
1 cup milk	12 oz. cooked young carrots
1½ oz. aged cheese	parsley
	1 oz. cornflakes

Saute the chopped onion in 1 tbsp. butter. Stir in the flour and gradually add the milk, stirring continuously until the sauce is thick and smooth. Stir in half of the grated cheese, salt, seasonings, the cooked sliced carrots, and finely chopped parsley. Turn into a buttered ovenproof dish. Crush the cornflakes, stir in the rest of the melted butter, cover the vegetables with it and top with the rest of the grated cheese. Put the dish into the top part of a pre-heated oven (325 degrees) for 20 minutes.

CUCUMBER AU GRATIN

1 large cucumber	parsley
2 large onions	celery salt
salt	1½ oz. aged cheese
pepper	1 tbsp. butter
thyme	

Peel the cucumber, cut it lengthwise, take out the soft center and cut the cucumber halves into pieces. Peel and chop the onion and mix with the cucumber. Stir in the salt and pepper with the finely-chopped herbs and put the vegetables into a buttered ovenproof dish. Cover with grated cheese, dot with the butter, put the dish into the middle of a pre-heated oven (400 degrees) and heat through for 30 minutes. The vegetables will then be tender and the topping light golden brown.

CAULIFLOWER CHEESE SPECIAL

1 cauliflower	Cheese Sauce:
2 lbs. Belgian endive	1 oz. butter
or 12 oz. celery	1 oz. flour
salt	1 cup milk
8 slices ham	salt, pepper
	seasoned salt
	ground paprika
	1½ oz. aged cheese

Boil the vegetables in a little salted water. Melt the butter for the sauce and stir in the flour. Add the milk gradually, stirring continuously, and only adding more milk when the sauce in the pan is smooth. Season with salt and seasonings, remove from the heat and stir in half of the grated cheese. Put the drained vegetables into an ovenproof dish and cover with the slices of ham. Pour the sauce on top and sprinkle with the rest of the cheese. Put the dish into the top part of a preheated oven (450 degrees) for about 15 minutes until the cheese is golden brown.

MUSHROOM FRICASSEE

1 lb. mushrooms	½ cup coffee cream
2 tbsps. butter	salt
1 onion	rosemary
2 tbsps. flour	chervil
2 tbsps. tomato puree	parsley
1½ cup bouillon stock	

Wash the mushrooms and fry them in the butter with the chopped onion. Sprinkle in the flour, stir in the tomato puree and gradually add the stock, stirring continuously until the sauce is smooth and thick. Cook gently for a few more minutes and then stir in the cream, salt and chopped herbs to taste. Before serving, sprinkle with chopped parsley.

MIXED VEGETABLES AU GRATIN

12 oz. cabbage	salt
1 onion	seasoned salt
1 green pepper	thyme
1 tbsp. butter	3 oz. aged cheese
2 tomatoes	

Wash the cabbage, slice it thinly and re-wash. Chop the onion and the green pepper. Braise the onion, pepper and cabbage for about 10 minutes in the butter. Peel and slice the tomatoes and stir into the vegetables. Drain and season to taste with the salt, seasoned salt, and thyme and place in a buttered ovenproof dish. Cover with grated cheese. Put the dish into the top part of a pre-heated oven (450 degrees) for about 10 minutes.

STUFFED TOMATOES

8 medium tomatoes	1 bunch parsley
½ cup smoked lean bacon	dash of salt
1 medium onion	pepper
9 oz. can mushrooms	butter for greasing

Cut off the tops of the tomatoes. Carefully remove the pulp, and lightly salt. Cut the bacon into small cubes and saute with the diced onions until glazed. Cut the mushrooms into leaves and combine with the finely-chopped parsley and seasonings. Stuff the mushroom mixture into the prepared tomatoes and set the tomatoes on a greased, heat-resistant pan. Make slits into the tops of the tomatoes cross-wise, cover the tomatoes and top with a dab of butter. Pre-heat the oven to 350 degrees and cook for 15–20 minutes.

HOT SPICY VEGETABLES WITH ONION

½ lb. smoked, lean bacon	black pepper
3 tbsps. butter	pinch of thyme
½ lb. peeled onions	juice from ½ lemon
5 peeled tomatoes	½ cup grated Edam cheese
1 cup milk	
pinch of salt	

Stew the cubed bacon in butter until glazed. Cut the onions into rings, tomatoes into cubes, and braise for 10 minutes. Pour in the milk. Add the seasonings up to the lemon juice and let the vegetables simmer on low heat for 10 minutes. Add the lemon juice and coarsely-grated Edam cheese. Season to taste.

DUTCH LENTIL HOT DISH

13 oz. lentils	pinch of sugar
3 cups water for soaking	black pepper
1 leek	2 smoked German sausages
½ celery stick	⅔ cup baby Gouda cheese
2 carrots	1 tbsp. butter
salt	

Wash the lentils and soften the night before in water. Boil ½ hour in the remaining water. Wash the vegetables and cut into fine strips or cubes, add them along with the spices and small sausages and cook everything thoroughly ½ hour more. Cube the Gouda cheese and slice the sausages. Blend into the vegetables, and season with a dash of vinegar and butter. Boiled potatoes go well with this.

ALGERIAN AUBERGINES (EGG PLANT)

2 large eggplants	½ tsp. paprika
⅔ cup ground beef & pork	½ tsp. anchovy paste
1 cup cubed Edam cheese	2 cups tomato sauce
black pepper	1 clove garlic
salt	2 tbsps. butter
1 bunch parsley	

Wash the eggplants, cut into half lengthwise. Remove ½ inch pulp. Combine the meat with the cubed cheese, seasonings, and eggplant pulp. Stuff into the eggplant and lay on a greased, heat resistant pan. Season the tomato sauce and pour over the eggplant, top with daubs of butter and cook thoroughly at 350 degrees for 25 minutes. Sprinkle with chopped parsley and serve with rice or noodles.

ZUCCHINI ROMAGNA

3 tbsps. butter	14 oz. zucchini
11 oz. pork	½ cup sour cream
1 onion	pinch of sugar
½ tsp. salt	1 bunch chives
½ tsp. cayenne pepper	4 slices middle-aged Gouda
½ tsp. oregano	
14 oz. peeled Italian tomatoes	

Heat the butter in a heat-resistant pan. Cut the meat into 1 inch cubes and cook until golden brown. Add the onions cut into rings, salt, pepper and oregano and briefly braise the thick slices of zucchini lengthwise over the top. Combine the cream with sugar and pour over the zucchini. Cover, and stew the vegetables on low heat for 20 minutes. Remove the rinds from the cheese and lay over the mixture; let melt for a few minutes. Sprinkle the top with finely-diced chives and serve with boiled grain rice.

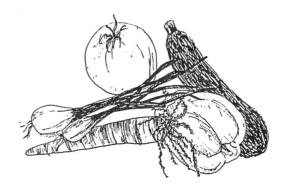

EXOTIC EGGPLANT DISH

3 tbsps. butter	3 eggplants
1 clove garlic	3 small zucchinis
salt	½ bay leaf
3 onions	½ tsp. cayenne pepper
3 fresh green peppers	1 cup white wine
4 peeled tomatoes	⅔ cup grated Gouda

Heat the butter in a heat-resistant pan. Dice the onions finely, rub in the garlic clove with salt, and brown both in the pan. Cut the peppers, tomatoes, eggplant and peeled zucchini into 1-inch cubes, and stew along with the onions and garlic clove for 5 minutes. Add the remaining seasonings, pour in the wine, and cook thoroughly on low heat for 15–20 minutes. Do not overcook the vegetables. Sprinkle heavily with grated cheese and brown briefly under the pre-heated broiler.

VARIEGATED VEGETABLE PLATTER

instant mashed potatoes	salt
(4 servings)	pepper
1 egg	10 oz. frozen peas
¼ cup grated aged Gouda	2 tbsps. butter
4 tomatoes	pinch of sugar
1 oz. grated aged Gouda	½ bunch parsley
10 oz. frozen green beans	
2 tbsps. butter	

Lay out a sheet of aluminum foil over a cookie sheet or broiling pan. Prepare the mashed potatoes as directed, and blend in the egg and grated, mature Gouda cheese. With a decorating gun, dollop small rosettes onto the baking sheet with the mixture. Wash the tomatoes and dry. Cut slits crossways into the tops. Pull back the skin and place the grated Gouda cheese in the open areas. Set on the cookie sheet next to the rosettes. Add butter and seasonings to the frozen beans and peas, wrap each in tinfoil, leaving the top uncovered and place them onto the cookie sheet with the tomatoes and rosettes. Set the cookie sheet with all ingredients in a pre-heated oven and bake at 350 degrees for 25–30 minutes. Sprinkle the peas with chopped parsley.

VEGETABLE-FILLED ONIONS

8 Stuffed Onions	Sauce:
Filling:	3 tbsps. butter
⅔ cup ground beef and pork	3 tbsps. flour
⅔ cup bacon	½ cup milk
chopped onion centers	1 cup water
3 eggs	pinch of salt
salt	pepper
pepper	nutmeg
paprika	½ cup aged grated Gouda

Peel the onions, wash and set into boiling saltwater. Boil for 25 minutes, let cool down and hollow out the centers. Combine the ground beef and pork with finely-cubed bacon, chopped centers of the onions, eggs, and the spices. Season the mixture to taste and stuff into the onions. In a frying pan, heat the butter and flour, and add the liquid. Season to taste. Pour the sauce in a casserole dish. Set in the onions, sprinkle with grated cheese and brown in a pre-heated oven for 30–35 minutes.

COTTAGE CHEESE PEPPERS

4 medium green peppers	½ tsp. paprika powder
9 oz. cottage cheese	1 peeled tomato
2–3 tbsps. milk	½ cup Edam cheese
juice from ½ lemon	1 hard-boiled egg
salt, white pepper	1 bunch chives

Wash the peppers, cut off the tops; remove the seeds and white ribs, and set into simmering saltwater for 8 minutes until almost thoroughly cooked. Let cool. Blend the cottage cheese with milk, lemon juice and the seasonings until smooth. Cube the tomatoes and cheese into small pieces, dice the egg and chives. Blend all ingredients with the cottage cheese. Season to taste, stuff into the peppers, and replace the top if desired.

MIXED CUCUMBERS

3 large onions	4 peeled tomatoes
2 fresh red peppers	dash of salt
3 large cucumbers for stewing	1 tsp. paprika
4 tbsps. butter	pepper
4 oz. can mushrooms	⅔ cup grated aged Gouda

Cut the onions in half, and peppers into strips. Pare the cucumbers, remove the seeds and membranes, and cut into 2-inch pieces. Stew these ingredients in heated butter for 15 minutes, and add a little of the vegetable water, if desired. Drain the mushrooms, and add, together with the tomatoes cut into eighths, to the mixture. Season, and stew for 15 minutes more. Blend in the coarsely grated Gouda cheese and serve sprinkled with diced chives.

BUTTERS AND SAUCES

European cooking is distinguished by its use of delicious and savory creams, butters and sauces. They can be used to flavor fish, chicken and red meat, as well as vegetables and breads.

Sauce Tips

—Prepare all light, thick sauces according to the recipe given below.

—Begin preparation with heated butter. Simmer flour until it is golden yellow and add as much broth and milk as needed by the recipe.

—A butter and flour sauce is called a Roux. With a roux base, the sauce can be made thicker or thinner by the addition of more or less liquid. It can be made richer by adding an egg yolk or cream.

—Pour in all liquids at once. Don't worry about developing clumps as a whisk will eliminate this problem.

Sauce Tips (continued)

—Boil the sauce gently but thoroughly to get rid of the flour taste.

—Thick sauces develop a "skin" coating when left out; this can be removed by adding a slab of butter over the top and stirring well before serving. You can also draw this skin off by using an egg yolk; beat the egg yolk well, add a little hot sauce and then fold down into the sauce.

—Melt butter for butter sauces slowly; do not let it bubble or turn brown.

—Butter sauces can only be kept for a short time.

—Butter that is molded into different shapes such as balls, flowers, slabs, etc. will not stick together when submerged in ice water.

—Herb butter should be stored in the ice cube tray of the refrigerator.

—Let ½–1 cup of butter soften at room temperature, then divide into 3–4 portions and season each differently.

SAUCES AND VARIATIONS

BASIC LIGHT SAUCE RECIPE

3 tbsps. butter
3 tbsps. flour
2 cups water
dash of salt

Add seasonings such as pepper, nutmeg, paprika, etc. depending on what dish they are for. Two cups of sauce serves 4 people.

Marnay Sauce
Prepare a light, basic sauce and enhance it with an egg yolk and a shot of cream of condensed milk. Finally whisk with ½ cup of mature Gouda cheese.

Tomato Sauce
In a frying pan, heat the butter and simmer the finely-diced onions and as described above, develop a light basic sauce. Add ½ cup concentrated tomatoes. Season with a pinch of salt and sugar, dash of thyme or oregano and ¼ cup grated mature Gouda cheese. You can prepare a mustard, horseradish or herb sauce by substituting those ingredients for the tomatoes.

DUTCH SAUCE

1 cup butter	dash of white pepper
3 egg yolks	or cayenne pepper
3 tbsps. water	1 tsp. lemon juice
pinch of salt	

Slowly melt the butter; if desired, skim off. Vigorously whisk the egg yolks and water in a double boiler. The mixture should be creamy and doubled in size from when you first began. While still beating, slowly add the butter. As soon as the sauce thickens and becomes heavy, season with spices. Serve immediately.

Note: Tastes exquisite with asparagus spears, broccoli, cauliflower, fennel and turbot.

Choron Sauce
Prepare the Dutch sauce. Blend in 1 tsp. ketchup and serve. Goes well with broiled fish, poached sole, stewed chicory and artichokes.

Mango Sauce
Prepare the Dutch sauce, and blend in 1 tbsp. mango sauce; serve immediately. Goes well with stewed fish and poultry.

India Sauce
Prepare the Dutch sauce and blend in 1 tbsp. curry powder. This sauce tastes delicious over chicken, stewed bananas and fishsticks.

Maltaise Sauce
Prepare the basic Dutch sauce, but instead of lemon juice, use 2 tsps. orange juice and the peel from ½ orange, cut into very fine pieces. This sauce is wonderful with beef.

BEARNAISE SAUCE

2 shallots	1 cup butter
1 sprig tarragon	3 egg yolks
3 peppercorns	pinch of salt
⅓ cup white wine	dash of cayenne pepper
¼ cup vinegar	1 tsp. lemon juice

Dice the shallots and tarragon finely, and boil with the crushed peppercorns in wine and vinegar, until the liquid is reduced to 1–2 tbsps. Melt the butter and whisk the egg yolks until creamy. Add the stock and spices. The Bearnaise sauce should be thick and can be served with fish, beef and eggs.

Mixed Pickle Sauce
Mix ½ cup lightly whipped cream with 4 tbsps. chopped pickles, 2 tsps. ketchup and season to taste with salt, pepper, seasoned salt and ground paprika to taste. You may substitute ½ cup sour cream for the whipped cream.

Peanut Butter Sauce
Mix 2 tbsps. peanut butter with 1 tbsp. ginger syrup, ½ cup sour cream, 1 tsp. Indonesian relish and salt to taste.

Soup Packet Sauces
Follow the directions of the packet of dried soup, but use only three-quarters of the amount of liquid recommended. Complete the sauce by stirring in 2 tbsps. of coffee cream or sour cream.

HOT SAVORY SAUCES

WHITE SAUCE

2½ tbsps. butter	salt
1½ oz. flour	pepper
2 cups milk	seasoned salt

Melt the butter, but do not let it brown. Stir in the flour and continue to stir until it forms a ball. Gradually add the milk, stirring continuously. Be sure that all the first addition of milk is absorbed before adding any more. Boil the sauce for 2–3 minutes and season with salt, pepper and other seasonings.

BROWN SAUCE

2½ tbsps. butter	worcestershire sauce
2 oz. flour	salt
2 cups bouillon stock	pepper
soy sauce	tabasco

Melt the butter in a small saucepan, stir in the flour and bake until light golden brown. Gradually add the liquid, stirring until the sauce is thick and smooth. If the sauce is not brown enough, add some soy sauce or worcestershire. Boil for 2–3 minutes, season to taste with salt, pepper and tabasco.

Curry Sauce
Use the basic recipe for the white sauce, but saute a finely chopped onion with ½ tbsp. curry powder in the butter, being careful that the butter does not brown. For the liquid, use stock from half a bouillon cube and half and half cream.

Paprika Sauce
Make the curry sauce, but use ½ tsp. mild ground paprika instead of curry powder.

Tomato Sauce
Make the curry sauce but stir in 2 tbsps. tomato puree instead of curry powder. Complete by stirring in chopped parsley, thyme and soy sauce.

Madeira Sauce
Make the brown sauce with 1½ cups stock and complete by stirring in 3 oz. madeira and 1½ oz. cream.

Sour Cream Sauce
Make the basic white sauce but use 1 cup stock and 1 cup coffee cream as liquid. Enrich with 2 egg yolks and 1½ oz. lemon juice.

Cheese Sauce
Add 5 oz. grated cheese to the white sauce recipe.

Parsley Sauce
See white sauce. Use stock made with a bouillon cube. Before serving, stir in 2 tbsps. finely chopped parsley and celery salt.

Mustard Sauce
See parsley sauce, but instead of parsley, stir in 2 or 3 tbsps. mustard. Season with salt, pepper, vinegar and sugar.

Red Wine Sauce
Make a brown sauce with 1 cup stock and 1 cup red wine. Season with ground cloves.

Melted Butter Sauce
Melt 3 oz. of butter in a saucepan, but be sure it does not turn too brown. Add a little salt, whisk well and serve in a gravy boat.

Brown Butter Meuniere
Brown 3 oz. of butter in a pan over medium heat, stir in a little salt and lemon juice, then pour over boiled fish, celery, fried fish, etc. Sprinkle with chopped parsley.

Clarified Butter
Melt the butter in a pan, but take care that it doesn't get too hot. Remove from the heat, let it stand so that the milk components can sink to the bottom. Pour off the clear butter and use it to shallow fry fine fish.

HOLLANDAISE SAUCE

parsley	½ tbsp. butter
crushed peppercorns	¾ cup Rhine wine
thyme	2 egg yolks
bayleaf	5 oz. clarified butter

Saute the parsley, peppercorns, thyme and bayleaf in butter for a few minutes. Add the wine, cook until half the liquid has evaporated and strain through a sieve. Put the egg yolks into a bowl and whisk briskly while adding the liquid. Thicken the sauce in a double boiler, then gradually add the slightly cooled, but still liquid butter concentrate while beating continuously.

COLD SAVORY SAUCES

STEAK SAUCE

8 oz. cottage cheese	1 tbsp. chopped parsley
1½ oz. milk	ground paprika
3 tbsps. ketchup	thyme
2 tbsps. madeira	worcestershire sauce
salt	pepper

Blend the cottage cheese with the milk. Stir in the ketchup and madeira and season with salt and other seasonings.

BULGARIAN SAUCE

1 clove garlic	1 tbsp. ground paprika
8 oz. yogurt	parsley
salt	

Crush the clove of garlic into the yogurt, stir in the salt, ground paprika and finely-chopped parsley.

RAVIGOTTE SAUCE

5 oz. mayonnaise	1 shallot
4 oz. sour cream	pepper
heaping tbsp. chopped herbs	celery salt
(parsley, tarragon)	

Blend the mayonnaise with the sour cream. Stir in the herbs and finely-chopped shallot, then season to taste with pepper and celery salt. To make a Mustard Sauce, replace the chopped herbs with plenty of French mustard to taste.

Remoulade Sauce
See Ravigotte sauce—add 1 tbsp. of finely-chopped sweet pickle, 1 tsp. of mustard diluted with a little lukewarm water and 1 tbsp. of capers.

GLOUCESTER SAUCE

3 oz. mayonnaise	worcestershire sauce
4 oz. sour cream	mustard
1 tbsp. finely chopped fennel	pepper
salt	

Blend the mayonnaise, sour cream and finely-chopped fennel, and season with salt and the other seasonings.

CHANTILLY SAUCE

1½ oz. double cream	lemon juice
¾ cup mayonnaise	salt

Whip the cream until thick, and fold carefully into the mayonnaise. Season with lemon juice and salt to taste. Serve the Chantilly sauce with asparagus, celery or cold salmon.

HOT SWEET SAUCES

CINNAMON SAUCE

1 oz. flour	1 tsp. ground cinnamon
1¼ oz. sugar	2 cups milk

Blend the flour, sugar and cinnamon with a little milk to make a smooth paste. Bring the rest of the milk to a boil and thicken it with the flour blend. Stir and cook gently for a further 5 minutes.

MOLASSES SAUCE

1½ tbsps. butter	2 cups milk
1 oz. flour	3 oz. molasses

Melt the butter in a saucepan. Stir in the flour and gradually add the milk, stirring continuously until the sauce is thick and smooth. Stir part of the hot sauce into the molasses, return to the pan, stir and blend well, but do allow it to boil.

RUM SAUCE

3 oz. molasses
2 tbsps. butter
1½ oz. rum

Stir the molasses and butter together in a pan over medium heat until the butter has melted. Add the rum and mix well. Serve with a hot pudding or with ice cream.

HOT CHOCOLATE SAUCE

8 oz. bitter chocolate
1¼ cup coffee cream

Dissolve the broken chocolate in the coffee cream over a very low heat, stirring until the sauce is smooth and thick. Do not over-cook as the sauce will become grainy. This sauce is excellent over vanilla ice cream and works well as a base for chocolate fondue.

CARAMEL SAUCE

1 oz. sugar	1 tbsp. coffee liqueur
1 cup milk	1 tbsp. chopped hazelnuts
1 tbsp. cornstarch	

Caramelize the sugar, quench with 1 tablespoon of cold water, add the milk and thicken with the cornstarch, blended with a little of the cold milk. Stir in the liqueur and nuts.

WHITE WINE SAUCE

1 cinnamon stick	2 egg yolks
3 cloves	¾ oz. brown sugar
peel of ¼ lemon	¾ cup of Rhine wine
2½ oz. water	3 oz. double cream

Simmer the cinnamon, cloves and lemon peel in the water for 1 hour. Pour through a sieve and cool the liquid. Beat the egg yolks and sugar until light and creamy. Gradually add the liquid and wine while continuing to beat. Thicken the sauce in a double boiler, stirring continuously—add a little of the hot sauce to the cream, return to the pan and blend well.

APRICOT SAUCE

½ jar apricot jam	1½ oz. Kirsch
2 tbsps. water	¾ cup coffee cream

Boil the jam with the water, cool and stir in the kirsch and coffee cream.

YOGURT SAUCE

8 oz. yogurt
1½ oz. fruit syrup
brown sugar

Beat the yogurt with the fruit syrup or sauce and sweeten to taste with the sugar.

COLD SWEET SAUCES

Cold sweet sauces can be served with both hot and cold puddings. To thicken sweet sauces, cornstarch is used. Sauces can also be improved by stirring in a dash of coffee cream.

Vanilla Sauce
Mix vanilla custard with milk until the sauce is of coating consistency.

Brandy Sauce
Flavor vanilla sauce with brandy to taste.

Chocolate Sauce
Dissolve ⅓ oz. cocoa and ¾ oz sugar in 1½ oz. hot milk. Cool and stir into 1 cup chocolate custard.

MARASCHINO SAUCE

½ cup double cream	red food coloring
1½ oz. maraschino liqueur	2 cups vanilla custard

Flavor the thickly-whipped cream with maraschino with a drop or two of red coloring and fold into the vanilla custard.

CONFECTIONER'S CUSTARD

4 egg yolks	2 cups coffee cream
3 oz. sugar	½ tsp. vanilla
¾ oz. flour	

Beat the egg yolks with the sugar until smooth. Stir in the flour and gradually add the hot cream which has been flavored with vanilla. Cook over low heat for 5 minutes, stirring continuously. Cool and use as required.

SAVORY SWEET AND SPICY BUTTERS

Drawn Butter
Blend 3 oz. butter with 2–3 tbsps. lukewarm water until smooth, stirring continuously. Add salt to taste and serve in a sauce bowl.

Tomato Butter
Stir one small can of tomato puree, salt, pepper, thyme and tabasco into drawn butter.

Parsley Butter
Stir 2 tablespoons finely chopped parsley, ½ grated small onion and celery salt to taste into drawn butter.

Garlic Butter
Mix drawn butter with a crushed clove of garlic, juice of ½ lemon, salt and cayenne pepper to taste.

Cheese Butter
Cream 3 oz. of butter and 3 oz. of aged cheese. Add salt and pepper to taste. To make a fluffy cheese butter, mix 1 egg yolk into the butter, season with a little lemon juice and fold a stiffly beaten egg white through the butter.

Shrimp Butter
Cream 3 oz. of butter well and then stir in very finely-chopped shrimp. Season with salt and pepper.

Blue Cheese Butter
Cream 3 oz. butter, mix with 3 oz. of finely-chopped Blue cheese and flavor with 2 tablespoons of Brandy.

Chives Butter
Beat ½ cup butter with a dash of salt and white pepper. Add in finely diced chives.

Mustard Butter
Blend ½ cup butter with a dash of salt and 2 tbsps. mustard.

Tomato Butter
Blend ½ cup butter with a dash of salt, 2 tbsps. of concentrated tomatoes and 1 tomato cubed finely. This butter is delicious on a cold roast beef sandwich.

Lemon Butter
Blend ½ cup butter and the peel from 1–2 unprocessed lemons, cut into very tiny pieces.

Dill Butter
Blend ½ cup butter with a dash of salt and 2 tsps. dill seed.

Herb Butter
Blend ½ cup butter, a dash of salt, 1 tbsp. of onion, finely diced, 1 tsp. of parsley, ½ ground garlic clove and 1 tsp. of lemon juice.

Horseradish Butter
Blend ½ cup butter with a dash of salt and 3 tbsps. of grated horseradish.

Garlic Butter
Blend ½ cup butter with 1 clove of garlic crushed with salt.

SWEET BUTTER CREAMS

HALF BUTTER

6 oz. butter
1¼ tbsps. water
salt to taste

Cream the butter with an electric mixer and then beat in the lukewarm water drop by drop, adding a little salt to taste. Continue to beat until all the liquid has been absorbed.

HONEY BUTTER

3 oz. butter
3 oz. liquid honey
lemon juice

Cream the butter and then add the honey very gradually. Add lemon juice to taste.

MOLASSES BUTTER

3 oz. butter
3 oz. molasses
lemon juice

Cream the butter and add the molasses very gradually, stirring until well-blended. Add a little lemon juice to taste.

CREME AU BEURRE

3 oz. butter	
3 oz. powdered sugar	
2 tsps. vanilla	

Cream the butter and add the sifted powdered sugar and vanilla. Beat well. It can be mixed with some custard for a less rich result.

COFFEE CREAM

3 oz. butter	1 tbsp. coffee cream
3 oz. powdered sugar	1 tbsp. rum
2 tsps. vanilla	

Blend butter, sugar and vanilla. Add cocoa and liqueur.

CHOCOLATE CREAM

3 oz. butter	1 tbsp. cocoa
3 oz. powdered sugar	1 tbsp. apricot brandy or
2 tsps. vanilla	Grand Marnier

Blend butter, sugar and vanilla. Add cocoa and liqueur.

COCONUT BUTTER

3 oz. butter	milk to mix
2½ oz. shredded coconut	lemon juice
3 oz. brown sugar	

Cream the butter, stir in the shredded coconut and brown sugar and add a little milk if necessary to make a smooth mixture, easy to spread. Stir in a little lemon juice to taste.

COFFEE AND MILK DELIGHTS

Milk, with its rich calcium content, is good for the teeth and bones, but it is not always the favorite beverage. Coffee, while it is always popular, could sometimes use a little lift to give it a fresh new taste.

Here then, are some coffee, milk and egg nog recipes which will help you to follow the meal with a unique and memorable treat.

COLD COFFEES

COFFEE MILKSHAKE

½ quart milk	3½ oz. coffee extract
¾ oz. brown sugar	4 ice cubes

Whisk the milk, sugar and coffee extract in a bowl or large jug. Pour into tall glasses and add the ice cubes at the last moment.

COLD COFFEE EXTRA

5 oz. milk	dash of apricot brandy
1 tbsp. instant coffee	1½ oz. lemonade

Pour the milk into a tall glass. Stir in the instant coffee and apricot brandy and top up with lemonade.

COFFEE FRAPPE

1½ cups milk	4 scoops vanilla ice cream
¾ oz. instant coffee	cocoa
¾ oz. sugar	

Put all the ingredients, except for the cocoa, into an electric blender and mix for 60 seconds. Pour the Coffee Frappe into tall glasses, sprinkle with cocoa and serve with straws.

COFFEE FLIP

3 eggs	1 tsp. vanilla
2 tbsps. instant coffee	1½ cups milk
2 tbsps. brown sugar	ground cinnamon

Whisk the eggs, together with the instant coffee, brown sugar and vanilla until it is light and frothy. Add the milk. Pour into wine glasses and sprinkle with ground cinnamon.

COFFEE FLIP DE LUXE

5 oz. strong coffee	1 egg yolk
¾ oz. sugar	3 oz. cream
1 scoop vanilla ice cream	4 ice cubes
1½ oz. cognac	6 oz. soda water

Whisk all the ingredients, except for the soda water, until light and frothy. Fill four glasses three-quarters full and top up with soda water.

RUM AND COFFEE FLIP

2 egg yolks	¾ cup milk
1 oz. sugar	3 oz. rum
¾ cup strong coffee	

Whisk the egg yolks and sugar until foamy, then mix in the coffee and milk. Whisk in the rum and continue whisking until the drink becomes light and frothy. Pour into four glasses and serve with straws.

COFFEE GINGER

⅔ oz. instant coffee	¾ cup ginger syrup
1 tbsp. sugar	½ cup double cream
8 cups milk	6 ginger sticks

Dissolve the instant coffee and sugar in the hot milk. Stir in the ginger syrup and chill. Pour into tall glasses, garnish with a big spoonful of whipped cream and top with chopped ginger. Serve with a long spoon.

ICED COFFEE

1 cup strong coffee	1½ oz. sugar
1 cup milk	½ cup double cream

Heat the coffee and milk, dissolve the sugar in it, then cool and chill in the refrigerator until very cold. Pour into 4 glasses and garnish with a spoonful of whipped cream.

WARM COFFEES

IRISH COFFEE

2 oz. soft brown sugar	½ cup double cream
1½ cup strong coffee	cocoa
¾ cup Irish whiskey	

Dissolve the sugar in the hot coffee. Pour 1½ oz. whiskey into each glass. Carefully fill to ¾ full with hot coffee. Pour in the lightly whipped cream over the back of a teaspoon and sprinkle cocoa on top.

CAPPUCINO

¾ cup strong coffee	cocoa, cinnamon, or nutmeg
¾ cup milk	sugar to taste

Make strong coffee and pour into small cups. Heat the milk and whisk until frothy and pour this into the coffee. Sprinkle with cocoa or ground cinnamon. Serve extra sugar separately.

COFFEE MEXICO

½ oz. cocoa	1½ oz. sugar
¾ oz. instant coffee	½ quart milk

Mix the cocoa, instant coffee and sugar. Add some of the cold milk and stir to make a smooth paste. Add this into the boiling milk and continue to whip well at simmering point for a few moments.

VIENNESE COFFEE

½ quart milk	1 oz. sugar
2½ tbsps. bitter chocolate	double cream
¾ cup strong coffee	

Boil the milk, dissolve the chipped chocolate in it and then stir in the coffee and sugar. When everything is well blended, pour into tall glasses and garnish with a whirl of whipped cream.

CALIFORNIAN COFFEE

1 orange	sugar
¾ cup water	whipped cream
¾ cup strong coffee	

Peel the orange and infuse the peel in boiling water. Add the hot orange extract to the coffee. Remove the peel and fill four cups with the mixture. Add sugar to taste and garnish each cup with a big spoonful of whipped cream.

FARMER'S COFFEE

½ tbsp. butter	ground nutmeg
2 oz. sugar	1 can beer
1 egg yolk	3 oz. brandy
1 tsp. flour	3 oz. coffee extract
ground cinnamon	3 oz. double cream

Cream the butter and sugar well. Stir in the egg yolk and then the flour, cinnamon and nutmeg. Beat in a little of the beer until foamy. Add the rest of the beer and bring slowly to a boil, whisking continuously. Let it boil for a short time, then remove from the heat and stir in the cognac and coffee extract. Pour into large cups or glasses and garnish with a whirl of whipped cream.

COFFEE VIENNA

2 egg yolks	2 tbsps. instant coffee
¾ oz. sugar	double cream
¾ cup water	cocoa
¾ cup milk	

Mix the egg yolks with the sugar. Bring the water, milk and instant coffee to the boil. Carefully pour a little onto the egg yolks, stirring continuously. Pour this back into the pan and cook gently until it has slightly thickened—do not boil. Serve hot in glasses. Pipe some whipped cream on top and sprinkle with cocoa.

PHARISEE COFFEE

1¼ oz. soft brown sugar	1 cup cream
1½ cups coffee	rum

Stir the brown sugar into the hot coffee and fill the cups. Spoon some whipped cream on top and cover with a dash of rum.

CLOISTER COFFEE

1 cup double cream	1 oz. soft brown sugar
⅓ oz. instant coffee	1½ cups strong coffee
⅔ oz. white sugar	3⅓ oz. Benedictine

Whip the cream, adding the instant coffee and white sugar gradually after it begins to thicken. Dissolve the brown sugar in the hot coffee. Pour the Benedictine into four glasses, fill up with hot coffee and garnish with a whirl of whipped cream.

MILKSHAKES AND EGGNOG

BUTTERMILK SHAKE

¾ cup buttermilk	1¾ oz. lemonade
1 tbsp. red fruit syrup	

Pour the buttermilk into a tall glass, whisk in the syrup and top up with lemonade.

FRUIT WHIP

1½ oz. brown sugar	juice of 1 lemon
3 cups milk	juice of 2 oranges

Whisk the sugar into the milk. Add the fruit juice, little by little, whisking all the time until thoroughly mixed.

BLACKAMOOR

3⅓ oz. yogurt	¾ cup lemonade
2 tbsps. coffee liqueur	brown sugar
2 cups vanilla custard	

Whisk the yogurt and liqueur into the vanilla custard. Pour into four tall glasses and top up with lemonade. Sprinkle with a little brown sugar.

CHOCO COCKTAIL

1 egg	3⅓ oz. orange juice
1 tbsp. brown sugar	2 cups chocolate milk

Separate the egg and beat the white until stiff. Cream the egg yolk and the brown sugar until frothy then stir in the orange juice. Mix this with the chocolate milk. Fold the stiffly beaten egg white into the drink or spoon on top as a garnish.

BANANA-PINEAPPLE SHAKE

4 eggs	¾ cup pineapple juice
1½ oz. sugar	1½ cup milk
2 bananas	

Beat the egg yolks and sugar until frothy. Reserve 4 slices of banana for garnishing and mash the rest. Add the mashed bananas to the egg yolks, whisk in the pineapple juice and the milk until the drink is light and foamy. Fold in the stiffly beaten egg whites and serve the shake in tall glasses.

LEMON SHAKE

juice of 2 lemons	¾ cup vanilla ice cream
1½ oz. brown sugar	1½ cup milk

Blend the lemon juice and sugar with the ice cream, add the milk and mix well. Pour into four glasses and put a slice of lemon onto the rim of each glass.

VANILLA MILK

3 cups milk
1 tsp. vanilla
juice of 1 lemon

Heat the milk and mix with the vanilla. Sweeten to taste with sugar.

HONEY MILK

4 tbsps. honey
3 cups milk
juice of 1 lemon

Dissolve the honey in the hot milk and add the lemon juice, drip by drip, stirring continuously.

MILK PUNCH

2 egg yolks	1 glass sherry
1 tbsp. brown sugar	grated nutmeg
2 cups milk	ground cloves

Beat the egg yolks and sugar until foamy. Bring the milk to a boil and pour it over the beaten egg yolks, stirring continuously. Whisk in the sherry and season with the spices. Serve in punch glasses and sprinkle a little extra nutmeg on top.

WHITE DEVIL

3½ oz. rum	
2 cups milk	

Whisk the rum into the ice-cold milk, and serve chilled.

BRANDY EGG NOG

1½ cups milk	3⅓ oz. French brandy
2 egg yolks	grated nutmeg

Mix the ingredients well. Pour the egg nog into glasses and sprinkle with grated nutmeg.

RUM EGG NOG

1½ cups milk	3⅓ oz. rum
2 egg yolks	grated nutmeg

Mix the ingredients well. Pour the egg nog into glasses and sprinkle with grated nutmeg.

CREAM ALEXANDER

1½ cups coffee cream	2 tbsps. creme de cacao
2 tbsps. cognac	2 eggs

Whisk all the ingredients together until the drink is light and foamy. Pour into tall glasses.

DESSERTS

European recipes are noted for their uses of delicious sweet creams as filling for pies, pastries and tarts. Creams are also eaten as desserts on their own. In this section we offer a wide selection of both cream fillings and creams that stand alone. While these creams are all made with the freshest natural ingredients, there is no way to get around the fact that they are high-calorie sweet-treats. The key, of course, is moderation. Save them for special occasions, enjoy them in small quantities, but do enjoy them occasionally.

Cream Tips

—Powdered sugar and softened butter blend easily and well.

—Pudding gives a butter cream a resilient texture and makes it firm.

—Never use ingredients for a cream directly out of the refrigerator. Bring all ingredients to the same temperature.

CREAMS FOR FILLING AND FEASTING

BASIC BUTTER CREAM MIXTURE

1 cup butter	¼ cup vanilla
3 eggs	¼ cup sugar

Whip the softened butter with an electric mixer until foamy. Whisk the egg with vanilla in a double boiler until a thick cream develops. Remove the egg mixture from the double boiler and keep on beating until cooled. Slowly combine with butter.

—Butter creams can be varied deliciously by adding different ingredients.

—For mocha cream, blend instant coffee with dry cream and add to the basic butter cream mixture.

—For chocolate cream melt a bitter chocolate bar in a few tbsps. milk and add to the basic mixture.

—For fruit cream, thaw fruit and set over a double boiler; whip butter and fruit until foamy. Be sure the butter and fruit are the same temperature, to avoid curdling.

—Curdled butter cream can be smoothed again by beating in 1–2 tbsps. sifted powdered sugar and briefly stirring the cream in a lukewarm double boiler.

RASPBERRY CREAM WITH "SPIRIT"

10 oz. frozen raspberries	2¼ cups milk
1 pkg. vanilla pudding mix	1 cup butter
2 tbsps. sugar	2–3 tsps. raspberry liquor

Empty the raspberries into a bowl and let thaw, covered. Make the pudding from the mix, sugar and milk, as directed on the package. Let cook, and stir it now and then to prevent a skin from developing. Whip the softened butter until foamy; then, with a tablespoon, add the cooled pudding and blend together. Set the bowl of fruit briefly in warm water, until the temperature is the same as the cream. While constantly stirring, add to the cream without liquid. Finally, spoon in the raspberry spirits with a teaspoon and beat the mixture well.

MOCHA CREAM WITH GRAND MARNIER

1 pkg. vanilla pudding mix	12 oz. instant coffee
2 tbsps. sugar	2–3 tsps. Grand Marnier
2¼ cups milk	dash powdered sugar
1 cup butter	

Make the pudding from the mix, sugar and milk as directed. Let cool; keep stirring to prevent a skin from developing. Beat softened butter with an electric hand mixer or whisk until foamy. With a tablespoon, add the cooled pudding mixture and blend with the coffee. with a teaspoon, add the Grand Marnier and beat well.

STRAWBERRY CREAM

11 oz. frozen strawberries	1 cup butter
1 tbsp. vanilla	dash powdered sugar
2¼ cups milk	

Empty the strawberries into a bowl and let thaw, covered. Make the pudding from the mix, vanilla and milk, as directed. Let cool; meanwhile keep stirring to prevent a skin from developing. Beat the softened butter with an electric hand mixer or a whisk, until foamy. With a tablespoon, add the cooled pudding mixture and blend into the butter. Briefly set the bowl of fruit in warm water, until the temperature reaches the same as the cream. Then, gradually add to the cream without the liquid, while constantly stirring. If you prefer a sweeter cream, add a little sifted powdered sugar at the end.

CHOCO CREAM WITH COGNAC

1 pkg. vanilla pudding mix	1–2 tbsps. milk
2 tbsps. sugar	1 cup butter
2¼ cups milk	2–3 tsps. Cognac
½ cup bitter chocolate bar	

Make the pudding from the mix, sugar and yolk, as directed. Keep stirring while it is cooling to prevent a skin from forming on top. Break the chocolate bar into pieces and let melt slowly with the milk. Beat the softened butter with an electric hand mixer or whisk until foamy. With a tablespoon pour in the pudding and the cooled chocolate and blend into the butter. Finally, carefully add the Cognac.

HONEY-CROQUANT CREAM

1 small pkg. vanilla pudding mix	3—4 tbsps. honey
2 tbsp. sugar	2 oz. bag croquant
2¼ cups milk	(roasted almond sugar
1 cup butter	for sprinkling)

Make the pudding from the mix, sugar and milk. Keep stirring occasionally while cooling to prevent a skin from forming on top. Whip the softened butter with an electric hand mixer or whisk until foamy. With a teaspoon, spoon in the pudding and honey and blend well.

ALMOND CREAM

7 oz. ground almonds	⅓ cup butter
⅔ cup sugar	4 egg yolks
2 tbsps. vanilla	1 oz. rum
2 tbsps. orange preserves	

Combine almonds, sugar, vanilla and butter well. Add egg yolks and rum; work through the mixture with an electric hand mixer or ladle.

MALAKOFF-CHARLOTTE

1 small pkg. lady fingers	½ oz. cherry liquor
½ cup butter	(Kirsch)
½ cup powdered sugar	pulp from ½ vanilla bean
½ cup ground almonds	1 cup cream
	maraschino cherries

Arrange the lady fingers on the bottom and edges of a pan or bowl suitable for this purpose. If you only want the lady fingers to be on the edges, lay a sheet of tinfoil or waxed paper on the bottom, cut to fit the pan. Whip the softened butter, sifted powdered sugar, ground almonds, cherry liquor (Kirsch) and vanilla bean pulp until foamy. Blend in the stiffly-beaten cream, pour the mixture into the pan and smooth. Let cool thoroughly, turn over on a platter, decorate with a little cream and garnish with maraschino cherries.

FINE CARAMEL CREAM

½ cup sugar	6 sheets gelatin
¼ cup butter	2 egg whites
½ cup water	6 tbsps. beaten cream for
1 cup milk	blending
2 egg yolks	beaten cream for garnish
2 tbsps. vanilla	
chocolate for garnish	

Heat the butter and sugar until golden brown. Then quench with water; add up to 2 cups milk. Beat the egg yolks and vanilla until foamy. Soak the gelatin and fully dissolve in 1–2 tbsps. boiling water, but don't let the gelatin boil. Combine the caramel milk, foamy egg yolks and dissolved gelatin well, and let thicken a little, until runnels form; fold in the stiffly-beaten egg whites and cream evenly, and pour the cream into small bowls. Chill and let set. Before serving, garnish with a dollop of cream and shaved chocolate.

SWEET WELCOME

1 can pear halves	1 egg white
4 tbsps. strong black tea	½ cup whipped cream
7 oz. bitter chocolate bar	few shots bitters
⅓ cup butter	2 tsps. Escorial
3 egg yolks	chopped almonds
1 tbsp. vanilla	

Drain the pears well on a sieve. Scald one level teaspoon tea with ½ cup boiling water; simmer. Break the chocolate into pieces, pour over the hot tea and let fully melt in the double boiler. Finally add the butter. Whip the egg yolks with vanilla until foamy. Gradually blend in the cooled chocolate mixture. Beat the egg whites and cream separately, until stiff; blend in a few shots of bitters and Escorial in the cream. Set the pear halves in cups or glass bowls, with the round side facing you. Pour the cream over the fruit and garnish with almonds.

CHOCOLATE MOCHA CREAM

12 oz. instant coffee	3 egg whites
3 tbsps. boiling water	¼ cup sugar
4 oz. bitter chocolate bar	½ cup whipped cream
⅓ cup butter	chocolate bar for garnish
3 egg yolks	

Dissolve the coffee in the boiling water. Set the bowl in the double boiler; add the broken chocolate. Add the butter to the almost-melted chocolate, stir until fully smooth and remove from the double boiler. Beat the egg yolks until foamy and blend the barely-warm chocolate mixture into it. Beat the egg whites with the sugar until very stiff; the whipped cream likewise. If desired, set a little cream aside for decorating. Pour both over the cream and whisk well. Pour into a glass bowl or glasses and cool slightly. Garnish with dollops of whipped cream and shaved chocolate.

VANILLA CUSTARD

2 eggs	3 cups milk
1½ oz. sugar	2 tsps. vanilla
1 oz. cornstarch	

Beat the eggs and sugar together, stir in the cornstarch and add as much cold milk as is necessary to make a smooth paste. Stirring continuously, slowly add the boiling milk, return the mixture to the pan and bring to a boil over a moderate heat. Cook gently for 2–3 minutes and then stir in the vanilla.

CHOCOLATE CUSTARD

1 oz. cocoa	1 oz. cornstarch
2 oz. sugar	2 cups milk

Melt the cocoa, sugar and cornstarch and stir in a little of the cold milk to make a smooth paste. Bring the rest of the milk to a boil, add the chocolate paste, and cook the custard over moderate heat until smooth and thick.

CARAMEL CUSTARD

3 oz. sugar	1 oz. cornstarch
3 cups milk	

Slowly heat the sugar in a frying pan until it is golden brown and melted. Remove from the heat, pour in 3 tbsps. of cold water, add 2 cups milk and dissolve the caramel in it over a low heat. Blend the cornstarch with the rest of the milk until smooth and thicken the caramel with the cornstarch blend.

CREAM CUSTARD

4 egg yolks	2 cups coffee cream
3 oz. sugar	

Beat the egg yolks with the sugar until light and creamy. Heat the cream and stir gradually into the egg and sugar. Put the custard into the top part of a double boiler and stir over low heat until thickened.

TRIFLE

4 slices cake	1 egg white
1 small glass sherry	1 cup vanilla custard
1 small can tropical fruit cocktail	½ cup cream

Put a slice of cake into each of the coupe glasses and sprinkle with sherry. Spoon the fruit cocktail on top. Beat the egg white until stiff and fold it carefully into the vanilla custard. Pour this over the fruit cocktail and garnish with a whirl of whipped cream and a few pieces of fruit reserved for this purpose.

COUPE NIEVE SOL

2 bananas	½ cup cream
1 cup chocolate custard	1½ tbsps. sugar
2 tbsps. raisins, soaked in rum	4 peach halves

Mash the bananas and beat in the chocolate custard. Add the raisins and pile into 4 coupe glasses. Whip the cream and the sugar until stiff and spoon on top of the banana custard. Cut the peach halves into quarters and arrange them like a sunflower on top of the whipped cream.

CHOCOLATE MOUSSE

1 egg	1 cup cream
1½ oz. sugar	½ glass Grand Marnier
2 oz. plain chocolate	fan wafers
juice of ½ lemon	

Beat the egg yolk and half the sugar until light and fluffy. Melt the chocolate in a double boiler and fold it into the beaten egg yolk and sugar. Beat the egg white until very stiff, adding the rest of the sugar gradually; stir in the lemon juice. Whip the cream until almost stiff, spoon it on top of the egg white, cover with the melted chocolate mixture and Grand Marnier and fold together carefully. Serve in coupe glasses and garnish with a fan wafer.

HONEY YOGURT

1 cup double cream	1½ tbsps. brown sugar
2 cups yogurt	cornflakes
3–4 tbsps. liquid honey	

Whip the cream and fold into the yogurt. Stir in the honey and the brown sugar. Pour into a custard bowl and sprinkle with cornflakes.

MOCCA MOUSSE

1 cup whipped cream	1½ oz. coffee extract
1½ oz. sugar	4 fan wafers

Whip the cream and sugar until almost stiff and fold in with the coffee extract. Serve in coupe glasses and decorate with a fan wafer.

LEMON MOUSSE

1 cup cream	4 tbsps. dry sherry or
1½ oz. sugar	dry white wine
1 tsp. vanilla	4 lady fingers
grated rind and juice of 1 lemon	

Whip the cream, sugar, vanilla, lemon juice and grated lemon rind until almost stiff. Carefully fold in the wine or sherry. Fill 4 coupe glasses and garnish with a lady finger.

TARTS AND PIES

Filled with the creams in the previous chapter or with fresh fruits, pies and tarts make delicious finishing touches to a meal. Because they can keep for several days, they also make lovely school lunch treats, excellent additions to family dinners and taste just as good cold as warm.

Pie Tips

—A spatula is ideal for lifting the bottom crust of pies as well as for smoothing cream into a piecrust.

—Pies can be filled with various creams as well as with well-whipped preserves that complement the cream.

—After setting the bottom crust into a pan, lightly indent the edges on all sides.

—Spread cream evenly over the surface and rim of the pie, rinsing the spatula in hot water in between; the surface will then be nicely smooth.

A decorating gun is wonderful for putting cream into a crust and for decorating. Squeeze the decorating gun to allow air to escape, pour in the cream and garnish.

APPLE TARTS

Batter:	Ingredients:
1 cup butter	2 lbs. apples
7 oz. sugar	3½ oz. raisins
2 tbsps. vanilla	¼ cup chopped almonds
grated peel from 1 lemon	2 tbsps. sugar
pinch of salt	¼ tsp. cinnamon
4 eggs	
1¼ cup flour	
⅔ cup cornstarch	
4 level tsps. baking powder	

Add the softened butter in a large bowl. In the order given, add the ingredients over the butter. Combine flour, cornstarch and baking powder, then sift. Work up a creamy batter with an electric hand mixer, mixing a few minutes. Pour ¾ of the mixture into a 10-inch greased pie pan. Fill the remaining batter into a decorating gun with a large icing tube, and create a rim. Reserve a little batter. Peel the apples, slice and blend with the washed and towel-dried raisins, almonds, sugar and cinnamon; arrange over the dough. With the remaining dough, top it off by using the decorating gun, squirting out lattice-like decorations. Bake in a pre-heated oven at 375 degrees for 90 minutes.

FILLED CROISSANTS

3 tbsps. butter	3 tbsps. four
2 large eggs, divided	3 tbsps. cornstarch
½ cup sugar (divided)	¼ tsp. baking powder
1 tbsp. vanilla	powdered sugar

Melt the butter and let cool. Beat the egg whites until stiff. Gradually add 3 tbsps. sugar. Continue beating until stiff peaks form. Whip remaining sugar with egg yolk and vanilla until creamy. Pour over the egg whites. Combine flour, cornstarch and baking powder, and sift over the egg mixture. Pour in the butter and blend everything with a whisk. Cover a baking sheet with aluminum foil, grease it, and spread 2–3 tbsps. of dough onto the tinfoil, forming circles at 4–5 inches. Bake in a pre-heated oven at 400 degrees until light yellow and roll together immediately into croissants. After cooling down, fill with raspberry, strawberry or mocha cream, and sprinkle with powdered sugar.

FILLED CHOCOLATE TARTS

Batter:	Filling:
1 cup butter	3 tbsps. candied orange
⅔ cup sugar	preserves
3 tbsps. vanilla	Icing:
pinch of salt	½ cup chocolate cake
4 eggs	frosting
1 cup flour	
½ cup cornstarch	
3 level tsps. baking powder	
7 oz. bitter chocolate bar	

In a large bowl, add softened butter, sugar, vanilla, salt, eggs, sifted flour, cornstarch and baking powder in the given order, using the electric hand mixer to develop a resilient dough. Grate the chocolate bar in the grinder or shredder in not-too-fine pieces and blend into the batter. Pour into a greased 10-inch pie pan and bake in a pre-heated oven at 350 degrees for 1 hour, 15 minutes. Let cool thoroughly on a rack. Slice through once and spread with the whipped preserves. Set on the upper half of the tarts and coat the surface and edges with melted chocolate frosting.

DUTCH APPLE PIE

1½ lbs. flour	½ cup raisins
½ tsp. salt	⅔ tbsp. rum
3–4 tbsps. water	½ cup almonds
1 cup butter	⅔ cup sugar
6 large apples	1 egg yolk for spreading
juice from 1 lemon	

Sift flour onto a cutting board. Add salt, and form a hole in the center. Pour in the water, set daubs of butter on the edges and chop through with a spatula. Then work through further with your hands, until a smooth dough is developed. Briefly chill. Peel and halve the apples, remove the core, slit the surface 3–4 times and sprinkle with lemon juice. Wash the raisins and moisten with rum.

Divide the dough and roll one half to fit a rectangular pan. Grease the pan and mold the dough into it. Wash the rinds, coat the bottom crust heavily with apples. Sprinkle with almonds, softened raisins and sugar. Roll out the other half of the dough into a rectangle, cover the apples with it. Pinch the sides together with the other dough. Brush with beaten egg yolk. Cut a few slits over the top to allow heat to escape, and bake in a pre-heated oven at 400 degrees for 50 minutes or until golden brown.

LINZ TART

¾ cup powdered sugar	pinch of salt
¾ cup ground almonds	pinch of ground clove
¾ cup ground hazelnuts	pinch of nutmeg
⅓ cup flour	2 dashes of cinnamon
1 level tsp. baking powder	grated peel from 1 lemon
2 eggs	red currant or raspberry
¾ cup butter	jam for filling
	1 egg yolk for brushing

Sift the powdered sugar onto a cutting board or table-top; add almonds, nuts, sifted flour combined with baking powder. Form a hole in the center and add the eggs; work up a dough and chill. Roll out ⅔ of the dough and cover the bottom and sides of a greased pan with it. Twist one portion of the remaining dough into a roll, lay on the edge of the bottom crust, mold into shape lightly with a fork. Pour in the jam; roll out the remaining dough and form narrow strips. Lay over the tart lattice-like and brush with egg yolks. Bake at 350 degrees for 50–60 minutes.

PUFF PASTRY TART WITH NUTS

1¼ cup flour	1 egg
¾ cup ground hazel or walnuts	¾ cup butter
¾ cup sugar	2 cups cream
2 tbsps. vanilla	2 tbsps. heavy cream
pinch of salt	nuts for garnishing

Sift the flour onto a cutting board; add the ground nuts, sugar, vanilla and salt. Form a hole in the center and add the egg. Set flakes of butter onto the edges. Work through with a spatula, then knead together. Chill the dough for 15 minutes. Roll it out and form into 4 equal bottom crusts; bake one after the other in a pan in a pre-heated oven at 350-400 degrees for 20 minutes. Beat the cream with the heavy cream, spread over the full-cooled bottom crusts and pile the crusts on top of each other. Put a dollop of cream on the surface and paint nuts over the surface.

CAKES AND PASTRIES

Delicious and unusual recipes for European cakes and pastries make this chapter a unique addition to your kitchen.

Cake and Pastry Tips

—Always combine flour, cornstarch, and baking powder and always sift, as that will make baked goods more spongy.

—A pinch of salt in cake and pastry doughs will improve the condition of the dough and will assure an appetizing brown color.

—Assume that eggs are medium in size unless the recipe states otherwise.

—Set pans and baking sheets onto the correct oven rack; high baked items like pound cake and boxed cakes should be set on the lower oven rack. Small baked items and baked goods that are in cake molds should be set on the middle oven rack; cakes on a baking sheet likewise.

—Cakes containing fruit should be topped with sugar only after baking. Cakes that are to be frosted should first be fully cooled.

—Freeze cakes and pastries without frosting. Frost them after thawing.

SHORT CRUST PASTRY

3 oz. butter	pinch of salt
¾ cup flour	¼ cup water

Cut the hard, cold butter into the sifted flour and salt with two knives until it resembles fine breadcrumbs. Add the ice cold water, little by little, until the dough forms a ball. Roll the dough out lightly onto a flowered board, turn the dough three times during the rolling. Flour it between turns. Fold up the dough and let it rest in a cool place. It is then ready for use.

PUFF PASTRY

3 oz. butter	pinch of salt
3 oz. flour	1 tbsp. water

Cut the cold, hard butter in large pieces through the flour, add the salt, and the ice cold water, little by little, mixing with a knife. Do not use more ice cold water than is necessary to keep the dough together. Flour a pastry board or table and a rolling pin, and roll out the pastry, lightly, until about the thickness of a penny. See that the pastry does not stick anywhere. Fold the pastry lengthwise and crosswise in three. Repeat this procedure twice more, and then put the pastry in a cool place to rest for 30 minutes. Roll and fold it three times, cool and rest and repeat this procedure once more.

FLAKY PASTRY

3 oz. butter	1 tbsp. water
3 oz. flour	1 tsp. vinegar
pinch of salt	

Cut the cold, hard butter into the flour with two knives, add the salt, the ice-cold water and the vinegar, mixing with the knives. Do not add any more water than is necessary to keep the pastry together. Roll out into a thin sheet on a floured surface and fold as for puff pastry. Roll out again thinly, fold and put the pastry in a cool place to rest for 1 hour. Roll out to the desired thickness for the recipe chosen.

SWEET SHORT CRUST PASTRY

3 oz. butter	salt
5 oz. flour	vanilla
2½ oz. sugar	grated lemon peel

Cut the butter with two knives into the sifted flour, then add the sifted sugar, a little salt and vanilla or grated lemon peel to taste. Knead all the ingredients quickly with a cool damp hand until the dough forms a ball.

VICTORIA SPONGE

5 oz. butter	3 eggs
5 oz. sugar	5 oz. flour
1 tbsp. vanilla	pinch of salt
or grated rind of 1 lemon	

All the ingredients should be at room temperature. Cream the butter, sugar, grated lemon peel or vanilla with an electric mixer for about 10 minutes, until light and fluffy. Add the eggs, one by one, beating after every addition and beat again for 10 minutes. Sift the flour with the salt and fold in until the batter is well mixed.

MOSCOW SPONGE

5 eggs	½ tbsp. cornstarch
3 oz. sugar	pinch of salt
3 oz. flour	3 oz. butter

Beat the egg yolks and sugar until all the sugar crystals have disappeared. Sift the flour, cornstarch and salt together into a bowl, then cut in the butter with 2 knives until it resembles fine breadcrumbs. Whisk the egg whites very stiffly, cover with the flour and butter crumbs and put the egg yolk mixture on top. Fold together lightly and carefully until well blended.

FRUIT CAKE

Batter:	3 oz. white grapes
7 oz. butter	3 oz. dried currants
½ cup sugar	¼ cup chopped almonds
2 tbsps. vanilla	2 tbsps. rum
pinch salt	
4 eggs	Frosting:
1 cup flour	1 cup powdered sugar
3 oz. cornstarch	2 tbsps. rum
2 level tsps. baking powder	2–3 tbsps. hot water
3 tbsps. finely-cubed, candied	few halved cherries
orange peel	
3 tbsps. finely-cubed, candied lemon peel	
⅓ cup finely-cubed, candied cherries	

Whip the butter with sugar, vanilla and salt until foamy; add eggs one after the other. Combine the flour with cornstarch and baking powder, sift and gradually blend into the mixture. Fold in the fruits, almonds and rum, and set the dough in a greased cake pan; pre-heat the oven to 375 degrees and bake for 70 minutes. Flip the cake over into a rack and let cool. Combine powdered sugar with rum and a little water until a thick mash develops. Spread over the cake and garnish with a few halved cherries.

POUND CAKE WITH AND WITHOUT FROSTING

Batter:	1½ tsp. baking powder
1 cup butter	powdered sugar
7 oz. sugar	
2 tbsps. vanilla	Filling:
pinch of salt	7 oz. bitter chocolate bar
4 eggs	
⅔ cup cornstarch	
7 oz. flour	

Whip the softened butter with sugar, vanilla and salt, until foamy. Gradually add the eggs. Combine cornstarch, sifted flour and baking powder, and gradually add to the mixture and stir. Pour the creamy batter into a cake pan lined with a greased wax paper, and baked in a pre-heated oven at 350 degrees for 60–75 minutes. Remove the cake from the pan, let cool on a rack and sprinkle with powdered sugar.

If you want to add filling, slice the cooled cake two times lengthwise and spread with the heavy melted chocolate. Fit the cake back together and sprinkle the surface with powdered sugar.

MADEIRA CAKE

5 oz. butter	3 eggs
5 oz. sugar	5 oz. flour
grated rind of 1 lemon	pinch of salt

All the ingredients should be at room temperature. Cream the butter, sugar, grated lemon peel with an electric mixer for about 10 minutes until light and fluffy. Add the eggs, one by one, beating after every addition and beat again for 10 minutes. Sift the flour with the salt and fold in until the batter is well mixed. Fold into a buttered and floured oblong cake pan and make a slight hollow in the center of the cake with the back of a spoon. Bake in the center of a pre-heated oven (300 degrees) making sure that the center of the cake is in the center of the oven for about 1¼ hours, until well risen and golden brown. To test the cake, spear the center with a toothpick, which should come out clean if the cake is ready.

SPICED MADEIRA

6 oz. self-raising flour	2 tbsps. mixed spice
5 oz. butter	pinch salt
5 oz. dark brown sugar	6 oz. currants or raisins
3 eggs	

Using the ingredients listed, follow the recipe for madeira cake (previous page) and stir in the currants or raisins. turn the mixture into a buttered, floured cake tin or ring mold and bake in the lower part of a pre-heated oven (325 degrees) for 1½ hours until cooked through.

ZIKA CAKE

5 oz. butter	juice and grated peel
5 oz. light soft brown sugar	of ½ lemon
2 eggs	2 large crisp apples
5 oz. flour	3 tbsps. apricot jam
pinch of salt	

Follow the recipe for madeira cake (previous page) using the butter, sugar, eggs, flour, salt, lemon juice and grated lemon peel. Quarter the peeled apples and slash the rounded side several times. Spoon the cake mixture into a buttered and floured spring release form and arrange the apples on top, round side up. Bake the cake in the middle of a pre-heated oven (325 degrees) for at least 60 minutes until well-risen and golden brown. Spread the warm cake with apricot jam.

CHEESE CAKE CRUMBLE

Crumble:	Filling:
1 cup self-raising flour	1 cup cottage cheese
5 oz. sugar	grated peel 1 lemon
1 egg	2½ oz. confectioners
2 oz butter	sugar
pinch of salt	1 tsp. vanilla
	2 tbsps. coffee cream
	1 egg yolk
	1 egg white

Put the crumble ingredients into a large bowl and cut with two knives until it resembles fine breadcrumbs. Put half into a buttered, flour spring release cake tin and press well against the base and sides. To make the filling, beat all the ingredients (except for the egg white) until well blended. Beat the egg white very stiffly. Fold the beaten egg white through the cottage cheese mixture and turn into the crumb-lined tin. Cover with the rest of the crumbs and bake in the lower part of a pre-heated oven (400 degrees) for about 30 minutes until golden brown and cooked through.

WALNUT LAYER

Pastry:	Filling:
4 oz butter	4 oz. sugar
5 oz. brown sugar	½ cup double cream
6 oz. flour	4 oz. walnuts
½ egg	½ egg
pinch of salt	

Using the ingredients listed, cut the butter with two knives into the sifted flour, then add the sifted brown sugar, a little salt and the ½ egg. Knead the ingredients quickly with a cool, damp hand until the dough forms a ball. To make the filling, melt the sugar in a pan over low heat until it is light brown. Add 1 tbsp. water—stirring continuously—and then a little of the warmed cream. Cook and stir until the caramel has dissolved. Stir in the chopped walnuts, spoon the mixture onto a buttered plate and cool. Grease a flan tin and press half of the dough into the base. Spread the filling on top and cover with the rest of the dough. Brush the cake with the beaten egg and bake in the lower part of a pre-heated oven (400 degrees) for about 40 minutes until golden brown and cooked through.

MINI APPLECAKES

Sponge:	Filling:
3 oz. butter	1 apple
3 oz. sugar	2 tbsps. raisins
pinch of salt	1½ tbsps. brown sugar
2 eggs	cinnamon
3 oz. self-raising flour	juice of ½ lemon

All the ingredients should be at room temperature. Cream the butter and sugar with an electric mixer for about 10 minutes, until light and fluffy. Add the eggs one by one, beating after every addition and beat again for 10 minutes. Sift the flour with the salt and fold in until the batter is well mixed.

For the filling, mix together the finely-chopped apple, raisins, brown sugar, cinnamon and lemon juice. Stir this carefully into the sponge mixture. Fill buttered and floured bun tins two-thirds full with this mixture and press any raisins that protrude back into the sponge to prevent them from burning. Bake in a pre-heated oven (350 degrees) for 20–25 minutes until well-risen and golden brown.

PETIT-FOURS

vanilla butter cream
mocca or chocolate butter cream
round biscuits

Using the creams from our cream chapter, pipe two different colors butter cream onto round biscuits. You will need two piping bags. Here are some ideas for garnish: Pipe a circle of vanilla cream onto a biscuit. Cut a second biscuit in half and place one half upright in the middle. Break the half into two and set them opposite each other in the middle so that you make four sections in all. Pipe a rosette of brown cream into each section. A simpler way is to pipe a little whirl of cream in the middle and to decorate it with half a nut, a tiny silver ball or candied cherry.

COOKIES

Easy to make, easy to eat, appropriate for every meal from weddings to picnics, cookies are favorites for family members of all ages.

ALMOND FINGERS

2 eggs	8 oz. flour
6 oz. brown sugar	3 oz. candied orange peel
3 oz. ground almonds	pinch of salt
6 oz butter	1 egg yolk

Beat the eggs and sugar for about 5 minutes with an electric mixer until light and frothy. Add the ground almonds and melted, cooled butter, beating for a further 5 minutes. Stir in the rest of the ingredients (except for the egg yolk) until well blended. Spread the dough out onto a buttered baking sheet, brush with beaten egg yolk and bake in the middle of a pre-heated oven (325 degrees) for about 30 minutes until golden brown. Cut into strips.

SPRITS

5 oz. butter	pinch of salt
6 oz. flour	1 tsp. vanilla
3 oz. brown sugar	

Knead the butter, flour, brown sugar, salt and vanilla well and shape into a ball. Beat until light and airy with an electric mixer. Put the dough into a piping bag and pump thick strips, zig-zag shapes or round whirls onto a greased baking sheet. Bake in a pre-heated oven (300 degrees) for 25–30 minutes for the large ones and 20 minutes for the small ones, until light golden brown.

CAT'S TONGUES

3 oz. butter	pinch of salt
3 oz. confectioners sugar	2 egg whites
1 tsp. vanilla	3 oz. flour

Cream the butter, stir in the sifted confectioners sugar, vanilla and salt. Fold in the beaten egg whites and the sifted flour. Put the dough into a piping bag with a plain nozzle and pipe strips 2 inches long onto a buttered baking sheet. Leave a little space between each biscuit. Bake in the center of a pre-heated oven (400 degrees) for 8–10 minutes until light golden brown and crisp.

CHATTERBOXES

2 oz. butter	2 tsps. ground cinnamon
6 oz. brown sugar	3 oz. almonds
3 oz. flour	1½ oz. water

Cream the butter, stir in the sifted brown sugar, the sifted flour, cinnamon and blanched and coarsely chopped almonds. Finally add the water. Mold into small mounds with the help of 2 teaspoons and place on a buttered baking sheet about 2 inches apart. Bake in the top part of a pre-heated oven (475 degrees) for about 4 minutes, and remove from the baking sheet with a palette knife while still warm.

CANDY CRISP

2½ oz. butter	pinch of salt
3 oz. self-raising flour	flaked almonds
1½ oz. brown sugar	coarse or candy sugar
½ tsp. ground cinnamon	beaten egg for glazing

Cut the butter into the flour with two knives. Sprinkle in the sugar, cinnamon and salt and knead into a smooth ball. Roll out the dough into a thick rectangle and place on a greased baking sheet. Sprinkle with almonds and coarse sugar or crushed candy sugar. Press in a little with a rolling pin and brush with beaten egg. Bake in the middle of a pre-heated oven (325 degrees) for about 20 minutes. Cool a little, trim the edges and then cut into rectangular biscuits.

BUTTER KISSES

5 oz. flour	pinch of salt
3 oz. butter	1 tsp. vanilla sugar
2½ oz. brown sugar	granulated sugar

Using the ingredients listed, except for the granulated sugar, cut the butter with two knives into the sifted flour, then add the sifted brown sugar, the salt and the vanilla. Knead all the ingredients quickly with a cool damp hand until the dough forms a ball. Roll the ball in granulated sugar and chill well. Using a wet knife, cut into slices about ½ inch long, place on a buttered baking sheet and bake in the middle of a pre-heated oven (350 degrees) for about 25 minutes until light brown.

BROWNIES

2½ oz. butter	6 oz. brown sugar
1½ oz. cocoa	3 oz. flour
2 eggs	3 oz. walnuts

Melt the butter and stir in the cocoa. Beat the eggs and sugar, mix the flour and chopped walnuts and stir into the beaten eggs and sugar, and add this to the butter-cocoa mixture. Spoon in small mounds on a buttered baking sheet and bake in the middle of a pre-heated oven (425 degrees) for about 15 minutes until crisp.

HAZELNUT BISCUITS

2 tbsps. butter	1½ oz. brown sugar
2½ oz. self-raising flour	1 tsp. vanilla
pinch of salt	½ oz. hazelnuts

Cut the butter into the flour with two knives and stir in the salt, sugar and vanilla. Knead into a ball with a cool hand. Chop the hazelnuts and knead them into the dough. Mold the dough into 12–15 small, equally-sized balls and put onto a buttered baking sheet. Press them flat with the palm of the hand. Bake in the middle of a pre-heated oven (350 degrees) for about 20 minutes until sand-colored.

SPRITZ SAND COOKIES

1¼ cup butter	grated peel from 1 lemon
1 cup confectioners sugar	1½ cup flour
½ cup cornstarch	3 oz. chocolate frosting
½–1 cup milk	almonds or candied
pinch of salt	cherries for garnishing

Whip the softened butter, powdered sugar and cornstarch until well blended, but don't beat until foamy. Add milk and the seasonings, then blend in the sifted flour. First develop into a dough with ½ cup milk; if it is too firm for shooting from a decorating gun, add more milk. It might be wise to bake a sample cookie or two. The cookie shapes can also be shot from a mincer or grinder, or with a baking gun. If using any of these appliances, the dough should be firm in texture. You can shoot curls, mini sticks, stars or s-shaped cookies. Garnish with almonds or cherries before baking. Shoot the dough onto a greased cookie sheet or lay the shapes onto the sheet and bake in a pre-heated oven at 375–400 degrees for 10 minutes, or until golden yellow. After cooling, partially or fully dip a few cookies in the chocolate frosting.

BUTTER COOKIES

1 cup butter	pinch of salt
½ cup powdered sugar	⅔ cup flour
2 tbsps. vanilla sugar	7 oz. cornstarch

Whip the butter with sifted powdered sugar, vanilla sugar and the pinch of salt, until foamy. Combine flour with the cornstarch, sift and blend ⅔ of it into the mixture; quickly knead under the remaining ⅓. Chill the dough for 30 minutes. Shape into rolls as thick as your thumb, divide into 1–1½ inch thick pieces, shape into balls, and lay on a floured cookie sheet. Flatten them slightly with a fork and bake in a pre-heated oven at 350 degrees for 13 minutes. They should remain very light in color.

LITTLE FRISIAN THUMBS

1 cup flour	1 tsp. ground ginger
¼ cup ground hazelnuts	pinch of salt
½ cup brown sugar	2 eggs
1 tsp. cinnamon	½ cup butter
1 tsp. ground anise	

Sift the flour onto a cutting board; top with ground nuts, sugar and seasonings, and dot the edges with butter. Chop through coarsely with a spatula, then knead the dough together and chill for 15 minutes. Roll out onto a lightly-floured dinner plate, cut into 1 x 2 inch strips and lay on a greased cookie sheet. Set into a cold oven and heat the oven to 350 degrees and bake for 40 minutes. The cookies are called "little Frisian thumbs" because they are lightly indented with the thumb when removed from the cookie sheet.

AMSTERDAM "PITMOPPEN"

1¼ cup butter	1½ lbs. flour
1¼ cup sugar	½ tsp. baking powder
2 eggs	1 egg yolk for spreading
pinch of salt	a few, shelled, halved
grated peel from 1 lemon	almonds

Whip the butter with sugar, eggs and the seasonings until foamy. Sift the flour with baking powder and work into the foamy mixture. Chill the dough thoroughly for 2 hours. Roll out until ¼-inch thick onto a floured dinner plate, cut into 1½ inch large squares and set apart from each other on a greased cookie sheet. Beat the egg yolk with a few drops of water, brush the cookies with it and top each cookie with 4 halved almonds into the shape of a star. Bake in a pre-heated oven at 375 degrees for 10–15 minutes, until golden yellow.

LOVE DIMPLES

½ cup flour	¼ cup butter
1 tbsp. cornstarch	1 egg yolk for spreading
½ cup ground hazelnuts	red currant berries or
¼ cup sugar	raspberries
1 egg	
grated peel from ½ lemon	

Sift the flour and cornstarch onto a cutting board; add hazelnuts and sugar. Form a hole in the center, and add the egg. Grate the lemon peel over the mixture and daub the butter onto the edges. Chop through with a spatula, knead the dough together and chill for 1 hour. Twist into rolls in diameters of ½ inch, cut off ½ inch pieces and shape into balls. Using the end of a wooden spoon or your finger, press deepenings into the balls. Brush the edges with whipped egg yolk and set onto a greased cookie sheet. Pre-heat the oven to 400 degrees and bake for 10 minutes, until golden brown. Let cool on a rack and add the raspberry or red currant filling while still hot.

SAND COOKIES

1¼ cup butter	1 tbsp. rum
1 cup sugar	1½ cup flour
2 tbsps. vanilla	1 tsp. baking powder
pinch of salt	
1 tbsp. milk	

Heat the butter, let it turn light brown and refrigerate. Whip the fully-cooled butter and gradually add the sugar, seasonings and liquid. Sift the flour with the baking powder, first blend the cream mixture and then knead the remaining ingredients. Shape into rolls of 1 inch diameter. Lay onto a platter or board and let them become firm in the refrigerator. Cut into ¼-inch thick slices, lay on a greased cookie sheet and bake in a pre-heated oven at 375 degrees for 10–15 minutes, until light in color.

CARAWAY COOKIES

⅔ cup flour	pinch of salt
½ cup mature grated Gouda	½ cup butter
1 egg yolk	1 egg yolk for spreading
dash paprika	caraway for sprinkling

Sift the flour onto a cutting board or in a bowl. Add the grated mature cheese. Add the egg yolk into the hole in the center of the flour. Spread the seasonings over it and set butter in small flakes on the edges. Briefly chop through with a spatula, then knead together the dough and chill for 30 minutes. Afterwards, sprinkle the flour on a board or platter, roll the dough out to ¼ inch thick and use the round or oval cookie cutters to form cookies. Lightly daub with egg yolk and sprinkle with caraway seed. Bake until golden yellow at 375 degrees for 10–12 minutes.

GOURMET DESSERTS

Now and again, it's fun to pull out all the stops and prepare a gourmet delight of a dessert to surprise family and friends. In this final chapter of our cookbook, we offer gourmet European dessert delights.

POMMES HENRIETTE

2 large apples	1 tsp. cinnamon
(Granny Smith's)	4 oz. sour cream
juice of 1 lemon	¾ oz. soft brown sugar
2 tbsps. butter	4 tbsps. ginger syrup
1 oz. sugar	8 pieces of stem ginger
2 tbsps. raisins, soaked in rum	1 oz. almonds

Peel the apples, core them and cut them horizontally through the middle. Place the halves, round side uppermost, in a buttered oven-proof dish and sprinkle with lemon juice. Mix together the butter, sugar, rum raisins and cinnamon and fill the centers of the apples with this mixture. Place the dish in the middle of a preheated oven (400 degrees) for 20 minutes. Beat the sour cream with the sugar, finely-chopped ginger and ginger syrup until smooth. Sprinkle the hot apples with toasted flaked almonds, and serve with the sour cream sauce.

STUFFED PEARS

5 fresh pears	3 oz. Blue cheese
or 10 pear halves	Dutch Brandy (Vieux)
lettuce leaves	black grapes
2 oz. butter	

Peel the pears, quarter them and remove the core or use pear halves from a tin. Line a round dish with washed lettuce leaves and arrange the pear quarters on top in the shape of a star. Blend the creamed butter with the finely-chopped Blue cheese and a dash of Vieux and pipe the mixture into the pear hollows. Garnish each half with a black grape.

BANANA ECLAIRS

Choux Pastry:	Filling:
3 oz. water	2 bananas
1¼ oz. butter	juice of ½ lemon
pinch of salt	8 tbsps. of advocaat
1½ oz. self-raising flour	1 cup double cream
2 eggs	3 tbsps. sugar
	2 tbsps. banana liqueur
Icing:	
1 tbsp. banana liqueur	
yellow food coloring	
3 oz. confectioners sugar	

Bring the water, butter and salt to a boil. Lower the heat, sprinkle in the flour and beat until the dough forms a ball in the pan. Remove from the heat and add the eggs one at a time. Beat for at least 2 minutes until the dough is smooth, thick and shiny. Fill a piping bag with the cooled mixture and pipe into 8 strips, 4 inches long through a wide nozzle onto a buttered baking sheet. Bake in a pre-heated oven (425 degrees) for about 20 minutes until brown and cooked through. Cool in the oven. Meanwhile, peel and slice the bananas lengthwise and brush with lemon juice.

Split the cooled eclairs half open, place a slice of banana inside, spread with a spoonful of brandy and pipe full with whipped cream (sweetened with sugar and banana liqueur) and close them up. Reserve a little whipped cream for the garnish. Stir the banana liqueur and coloring into the sifted icing sugar, drop by drop, and beat until thick and smooth. Spread the icing on top of the eclairs and pipe a strip of whipped cream along it.

Apricot eclairs can be made in the same way. Sprinkle the canned apricots with apricot brandy if wished and top with confectioner's custard. Pipe the whipped cream on top as a garnish. Icing is not necessary.

SAVARIN

Yeast Culture:	Sugar Syrup:
3 oz. flour	1½ oz. water
1 tbsp. fresh yeast	2½ oz. sugar
¾ cup milk	4 tbsps. apricot brandy or rum
Dough:	
2 eggs	Filling:
5 oz. flour	stewed or fresh fruit
⅓ oz. salt	double cream
2 tbsps. melted butter	
1¼ oz. brown sugar	
grated peel 1 lemon	

Prepare the yeast culture with the flour, yeast and milk. Sift the flour into a small bowl, pour the yeast, diluted with a little milk into a hollow in the top of the flour and stir in the rest of the milk, from the center outwards, until the batter is smooth. Cover and allow to rise for 15 minutes in a warm place (for example on the oven door with the oven set on warm).

Mix in the egg, 5 oz. of flour, salt, melted and cooled butter, brown sugar and the grated lemon peel. Knead together until the dough is smooth, working it until bubbles form in the dough—let it rise again for 30 minutes. Turn into a buttered ring mold filling it two-thirds full. Let it rise for another 5 minutes.

Bake the savarin in the center of a pre-heated oven (425 degrees) for 20–25 minutes. Test with a toothpick to see if it is cooked through. The needles should come out of the savarin quite clean. Turn out and cool on a cake rack.

Dissolve the sugar in the hot water, stir in the apricot brandy or rum. Pour the syrup into the ring mold and replace the warm savarin. Let the syrup soak into the savarin for about 30 minutes. Turn out and fill with stewed fruit or fresh fruit and garnish with whirls of whipped cream.

RUSSIAN TURBON

½ cup butter	2 tbsps. vanilla
3 eggs divided	⅔ cup flour
grated peel from ½ lemon	¼ cup raisins
pinch of salt	¼ cup finely-cubed
7 oz. sugar	candied lemon peel

Melt the butter and chill again. Whip the egg yolks with 3 oz. sugar, lemon peel and salt until foamy. Beat the egg whites with the remaining sugar and vanilla until very stiff and set on top of the egg yolk mixture. Sift the flour over the mixture, pour in the cooled butter and top with fruits. Carefully blend everything together and pour into a greased, smooth bundt pan. Bake in a pre-heated oven at 350 degrees for 40–45 minutes. Flip over onto a rack and let cool.

LADY MARY

1½ oz. sugar	4 pear halves
3 tbsps. apricot brandy	2 cups vanilla ice cream
pat of butter	3 oz. double cream
1½ oz. pear juice	1 oz. bitter chocolate
juice of ½ lemon	

Heat the sugar and 1 tablespoon of the apricot brandy in a frying pan or flambe pan. Stir in the butter and carefully carmelize over a low heat. Gradually add the pear and lemon juice. Continue to stir until the sugar has dissolved. Put the pear halves into the caramel sauce and simmer for about 5 minutes. Flambe with the remaining apricot brandy. Arrange the warm pears on top of the ice cream, pour the sauce on top and garnish with whipped cream and grated chocolate.

CERISES FLAMBEES

1¼ tbsp. butter	2 cups vanilla ice cream
1 7½ oz. sugar	1½ tbsps. sugar
2 cups pitted cherries	½ cup double cream
¾ cup Kirsch	

Melt the butter in a frying or flambe pan, stir in the sugar and gradually add ½ oz. of the cherry juice. Heat and stir until the sugar has dissolved. Add ½ oz. Kirsch, stir until warmed through, add the cherries and heat through. Flambee with the rest of the cherry liqueur. Serve the ice cream on 4 small dessert plates, top with the hot cherries and juice. Serve a bowl of sweetened whipped cream separately.

BAKED ALASKA

1 madeira cake	1¼ oz. sugar
3 oz. rum	4 cups vanilla ice cream
6 egg whites	3 oz. chopped hazelnuts

Slice the cake and line the base of a flat ovenproof dish with one third of it. Dilute the rum with a dash of water, and sprinkle on top of the cake. Beat the egg whites very stiffly, and fold in the sugar. Quickly put the ice cream on top of the cake and sprinkle with the chopped hazelnuts.

Cover the top and sides with the rest of the cake so that the ice cream is completely covered and sprinkle with the rum. Spread part of the stiffly beaten egg whites on the top and sides of the cake and pipe on the rest as decoration. Place the dish in the upper part of a pre-heated oven (500 degrees) for about 5 minutes or under a pre-heated grill (about 3 minutes) until the egg white is set and golden brown. Pour the rest of the undiluted rum into a ladle, warm it over a gas flame, light up the rum and pour over the Baked Alaska. Bring it flaming to the table.

STUFFED MELON

1 pineapple	1 lemon
1 small can fruit cocktail	brown sugar
1 small can mandarin oranges	walnuts
1 cup grapes	1 cup double cream
Grand Marnier	

Cut the top off the melon. Remove the fruit pulp and using a melon baller scoop out small balls and drain them well. Halve and de-seed the grapes, then mix them with a dash of Grand Marnier, the juice from the lemon and brown sugar to taste. fill the melon with the fruit salad, and sprinkle with chopped walnuts. Replace the top and secure with wooden cocktail sticks, but do not close it completely—the filling should be visible. Whip the cream until thick but not stiff and serve separately.

INDEX

Outstanding Books on Health And Natural Healing From Fischer Publishing

How To Fight Cancer And Win by William L. Fischer

It clearly spells out real cancer preventives and cures, many never before published, with strong scientific documentation and stories of miraculous cures. They are all presented in a concise, easy-to-understand style. You can put this vast knowledge into practice to ensure that this deadly disease never strikes home.

ISBN 0-915421-07-0...................................... $16.95

The Miracle Healing Power Through Nature's Pharmacy by William L. Fischer

Now you can learn how to treat virtually every disease or condition known to man—naturally! A comprehensive guide to help you and heal you... the most complete... most useful... and most up-to-date work of its kind. Complete with many documented case histories and 32 full-color illustrations.

ISBN 0-915421-04-6...................................... $19.95

How To Survive In The Hospital by Joan Haas-Unger, R.N.

There are too many procedures, performed by too many doctors, in too many places, with too high a stroke and death rate. This landmark book can help you lower your risks and increase you chances of survival in the hospital.

ISBN 0-915421-06-2...................................... $12.95

Hidden Secrets Of Super Perfect Health At Any Age Book II by William L. Fischer

Contains never-before-published health-related information with an incredible number of alternatives for treating everything from cancer to insomnia, from prostate problems to male impotency, from varicose veins to migraine headaches. Brings hope to sufferers of colitis, arthritis, bronchitis, asthma, heart problems, poor circulation and more. 288 pages.

ISBN 0-915421-05-4..$14.95

Miraculous Breakthroughs for Prostate and Impotency Problems by William L. Fischer

Good news for every man who has prostate or occasional impotency problems. This book describes in detail many of the latest therapeutic discoveries from Europe and America that can prevent, relieve or cure prostate disease, without the agony of prostate surgery. The book also discusses other male problems like testicle diseases, cancer, and the subject of impotency with honesty and sensitivity. **(Special Hard Cover Library Edition)**

ISBN 0-915421-12-7..$22.95

Mysterious Cause Of Illness and How To Overcome Every Disease From Constipation to Cancer by Dr. John Matsen, N.D.

Famed Canadian doctor uncovers the mysterious *REAL* cause of illness—and shows you how to overcome every disease from constipation to cancer. Dr. Matsen's acclaimed food-based "miracle cures" use *no* drugs, *no* surgery. They simply turn on the natural "internal healing power" built into every human body. Here is a safe, easy approach to health and longevity that has cured many "hopeless" cases after conventional medicine has failed! If you read nothing else, read Dr. Matsen's new revelations of secret remedies.

ISBN 0-915421-09-7..$16.95

Eye Secrets To Better Sight
by William L. Fischer

This important new book discusses the latest natural treatments for most common eye diseases. The author presents symptoms of various eye conditions from cataracts and glaucoma to macular degeneration, from the rare to the common place. He describes the warning signs of numerous eye problems and how to cope with them successfully. Also covered is the very latest in medical technology and explains how new procedures can cure most common sight defects forever. A must to read for everyone who cares about their eyesight—your window to the world—and that of your loved ones.

ISBN 0-915421-14-3......................................$16.95

Women's Secrets To Better Health
by Hanne Kramb, N.D.

This book was written to help women not only understand their bodies more fully, but show them effective means to increase their health. There are simple ways to ease premenstrual problems every month—naturally. There are nutritional treatments which help alleviate the discomfort of menopause. It also describes natural treatments for migraine headaches, depression, insomnia and stress. Other important health topics of concern to women in this volume are arthritis, osteoporosis, vaginitis, urinary tract infections and cancer. You'll be surprised how great you can feel by following these simple suggestions found in this new breakthrough book. Must reading for all ages.

ISBN 0-915421-16-X $19.95

Breakthrough in Arthritis
by William L. Fischer

If you thought there was nothing you could do for your painful condition, you need to read this book and discover freedom from arthritic pain. Learn more about the complex of nearly one hundred often crippling diseases called arthritis, such as rheumatism, bursitis, gout, carpel tunnel syndrome and more. Sound, natural, safe remedies are offered in detail. Also described in this book is the newest breakthrough formula of a leading world authority on arthritic pain.

ISBN 0-915421-15-1...................................... $14.95

The Romance of Creative Healthy Cookery
by William and Trudy Fischer

We know you'll fall in love with this book, because over 800,000 European families already have. All of the recipes are either time-tested European classics or inventive new dishes created by health minded experts and chefs. They have been adapted for ingredients that can be easily purchased at your local grocery store. Extra features include calcium-rich recipes to fight osteoporosis, nutritious vegetable dishes, budget meals fit for royalty and think lite... cook lite... eat lite recipes.

ISBN 0-915421-11-9...................................... $18.95

Shipping/Handling $3.00 for one book.
Additional books $1.00 each.

Fischer Publishing
374 Newton St, Box 368
Canfield, Ohio 44406
(216) 533-1232